The Art of Collecting Modern Art

The Art of

Collecting

Modern Art

Edward B. Henning

THE CLEVELAND
MUSEUM OF ART

Copyright 1986 by

The Cleveland Museum of Art

All rights reserved

Printed in the United

States of America

ISBN: 0-910386-85-4

The Cleveland Museum of Art

February 12 — March 30, 1986

Collectors who graciously lent works to the
exhibition were Mr. and Mrs. Heinz Eppler,
Mr. and Mrs. Frank H. Porter, Mr. and Mrs.
Edwin M. Roth, and six others who prefer
to remain anonymous.
The Eppler Family Foundation, Inc., made
a generous contribution toward the
production of the catalogue.
The exhibition received support from the
Ohio Arts Council.

Foreword

Collecting contemporary art—that is, the art of one's own day—is as difficult as it is exciting. In general, based upon observing what proved truly contemporary with each successive generation during the past century, the significant artists are those who are in advance of their times in perceiving the issues of the day. How extraordinary, for example, that the group of New York artists, now called the Abstract Expressionists, who quickly became international leaders in the years immediately following the euphoria of victory at the end of World War II were those whose work reflected the chaos and the dramatic change in values that within a decade were recognized as keynotes to understanding postwar America. To choose among the great number of artists working in the United States and abroad today is, therefore, a challenge if one's goal is to discover those who are truly (to use a popular, current expression) at the "cutting edge" rather than those whose work may merely be pleasing to live with.

Basically, there are two approaches to collecting contemporary art. One is to let the excitement of a generation's initial impact pass and the next generation emerge, perhaps a period of twenty years or so: then the leaders of that earlier generation become more clearly evident, as does their evolution, so that one is able to choose with greater conviction salient masterpieces. This has tended to be the policy of The Cleveland Museum of Art—certainly a reasonable one for an art museum devoted to all of the history of art rather than to modern art alone. Numerous private collectors also acquire successfully in this fashion.

The other approach is to make one's judgments even as the work is being created and to acquire accordingly. This is the more daring when one realizes that a work that seemed to have promise may not live up to expectations, whereas a work that appeared merely interesting may in fact become a leadership statement.

To delve into the area of the very new takes courage and judgment—even abandon—as well as an innate, sound taste that can readily free itself of the judgments of the past. Such collectors are few in number. One thinks, for example, of Mrs. H. O. Havemeyer, the three Steins, Peggy Guggenheim, or, more recently, the Rockefellers and the Tremaines; each justly deserves the accolades accorded them in later years.

Understandably—given its modest activity in acquiring modern works—The Cleveland Museum of Art follows with great interest the achievements of the area's private collectors. No one has done this more thoughtfully than Edward B. Henning, for twenty-three years the Museum's curator of modern art. In 1972 and again in 1980 he created impressive exhibitions of contemporary art drawn entirely from Cleveland collectors; it seems particularly appropriate, therefore, that this kind of exhibition mark the end of his full-time commitment to the Museum. (His final undertaking is the cataloging in depth of the Museum's modern collection, which is so much his achievement.)

The result of his quest is an eye-opening experience. Certainly the exhibition is representative of the imagination of those collectors who so generously agreed to cooperate. All of the works exhibited are being shown for the first time at this Museum. However, the rich and diverse private collections in Cleveland are such that another person might well choose different works from the collections represented here or even works of other collectors; but this is Ed Henning's exhibition. One sees readily how much we all owe to his astute judgment.

The reward of presenting this exhibition is the realization that collecting contemporary art in Cleveland is a far more active and varied pursuit than is generally recognized. One can only hope that the recognition of such healthy activity will become an example to others.

Evan H. Turner, *Director*

The title of this exhibition suggests that collecting art can itself be a creative activity. The Chinese recognized this centuries ago when connoisseurs began collecting the paintings of earlier Chinese masters; subsequently, the seals that the great connoisseur-collectors affixed to paintings enhanced their value almost as much as those of the great artists.

In my view, the collector of modern art has a greater opportunity to exercise taste and judgment than the collector of traditional art. Although it takes knowledge about when, where, and how to acquire Rembrandts or Van Goghs—and a lot of money—the joy of exploring uncharted territory alongside artists who are developing new modes of expression is not part of the experience of the collector of traditional art. The collector of modern art therefore takes risks but may enjoy the greater satisfaction of ''adventuring,'' in addition to the significant one of appreciating.

A general art museum, like the Cleveland, must collect in many fields. In all areas except modern, however, the works of art that exist are all that will ever exist. Modern art, on the other hand, is an open-ended, expanding area. New artists, new styles, and new works of art are constantly being introduced, and no museum has enough time and money to keep abreast of all of them. It is therefore necessary to select from the welter of new works the few that are believed to have aesthetic value that will last.

Inevitably, some mistakes are made, some important works of art are missed. This is where the intrepid collector can help the museum while collecting for his own satisfaction: he or she can take greater risks than the museum. And even if the over-all record is not as good as a museum's (although it often is), the individual may have some spectacular successes. Beyond this, if the collector loans or eventually presents these works to the museum, everyone benefits—particularly the public.

Thus, a concerned and active group of collectors of modern art provides essential support for a museum's program of collecting in an area little understood or appreciated by many people. Museums owe a debt of gratitude to these collectors, especially when they generously loan works for an exhibition.

While most of the lenders to this exhibition are old friends who have lent to previous shows, there are a few new lenders; some have elected to remain anonymous, however.

I thank the director of the Cleveland Museum, Evan H. Turner, for his encouragement and advice as well as permitting me complete freedom in organizing the exhibition. I also thank the trustees for granting me the necessary time and funds to do the exhibition. So many staff members have been so helpful that it is impossible to list them all. I must, however, mention the Registrar and his staff, the Photography Studio, the Print Shop, the Publications Department, the Department of Public Information, the Department of Building and Grounds, the Museum Designer, the Conservators, and the Department of Education. I especially wish to thank Tom Hinson, Curator of Contemporary Art; William Robinson, Assistant in Modern Art, who did most of the real work involved in mounting the exhibition; and Pat Krohn, Secretary for the Department of Modern Art, who kept us all running on the right track, and on time, and who typed innumerable manuscripts and lists. Above all, I thank the lenders to the exhibition.

Collecting art intelligently involves much more than having enough money; many people have the money, but few assemble great collections. Collecting art successfully requires knowledge, taste, and judgment as well as sufficient funds. It may not require the same skills used to create works of art, but it does depend on a comparable level of taste and judgment.

Collecting important modern art is expensive only if you can't afford it; if you can, it's a bargain. While the market value of a work of art varies according to fashion, its aesthetic value is determined by the inherent quality of the work. Once a particular work is acquired by someone who has a deep appreciation of it, the monetary value is not important to that person: only its aesthetic value matters.

Great art—painting, sculpture, music, drama, and other visual and performing arts—both reflects and determines the character and cultural level of a society. We do not revere ancient Athens or Renaissance Florence, for example, because of their material riches or their successes in battle, but because of their philosophers and artists. Plato, Phidias, Dante, and Leonardo are better known—and more important to us—than Phocion or Raimondo Montecuccoli. Pericles and the Medici are as famous as the artists they supported only because they supported them. They, and others who acquire works of art because they love them, are far more important to the human race than persons concerned only with gaining wealth and power. Indeed, it is the interest and commitment of great collectors that insures that the best fruits of man's creative capacities will be preserved and passed on to future generations.

There are different ways to proceed in collecting art. The collector who thinks only in terms of art that will appreciate in value is really involved with the art market rather than with art per se. However, since no one wants to invest considerable time and money in acquiring art that will not at least hold its value, how can the collector deal with this problem?

First, it is important to recognize that there are no guarantees. Second, the collector must differentiate between long-term and short-term market value. Anyone who wants to make a profit in a relatively short period of time should study the most popular dealers and critics, for it is they who create the market. Indeed, fashionable collectors usually follow the example and advice of fashionable dealers and critics. One might make money in four or five years this way, but one may never know the joy of living with great works of art, much less contributing to the culture of one's time.

Collectors who are genuinely concerned with art, and therefore with human values, however, will acquire only those works of art that they love and believe in. Such collectors will study art rather than fashionable trends. And when they are moved by a work of art and convinced of its quality, they will acquire it. Works acquired in this manner may or may not increase in dollar value in a few years' time; but they will probably maintain—or perhaps even increase—their value over a long period of time because the collector is involved with inherent aesthetic values rather than transient fashions.

The latter is the kind of collector that a museum appreciates: one who provides enlightened support, stability, informed opinion, and encouragement. In addition, this collector does not try to push the museum into rash adventures in collecting and exhibiting. For example, some museums have storage areas overflowing with works of art of little or no importance due to the influence—and frequently the generosity—of over-eager collectors.

The Cleveland Museum of Art is extraordinarily fortunate to have the support of many collectors who are primarily concerned with the quality of a work rather than with what they think will be ''popular.'' Beyond that single, unifying principle, collectors from this area, including the lenders to this exhibition, have varying approaches. Some acquire recent art, others specialize in the art of earlier periods or movements, and still others acquire various kinds of modern art. Some add to their collections slowly, carefully weighing each possible acquisition against several others before making a decision.

Others buy more rapidly, depending on their instincts. No matter what procedure they follow, however, quality is their main concern. (It would be interesting to compare these collections and to infer from them the particular attitude of each collector; however, many of the collectors prefer to remain anonymous.)

No one style or movement dominates the art scene today; instead, many styles compete for the attention of critics, collectors, and the public. The collector's challenge is to decide which movements, styles, artists, and works of art have significance and value, and which are relevant not just for today's culture but for all humanity.

The exhibition covers twentieth-century art from 1909 to the early 1980s and includes paintings, sculptures, and drawings borrowed from nine private collections. Although far from comprehensive, it nevertheless presents important works by leading artists of the period.

The Cleveland Museum of Art is most grateful to the collectors who generously supported this exhibition and to the many others who have supported past exhibitions and who remain willing to help. May their numbers increase.

Frank Auerbach, German, b. 1931
Primrose Hill, 1978 (fig. 47)
Oil on canvas, 45 x 60 inches (114.3 x 152.4 cm); Private Collection

Milton Avery, American, 1885-1965
Purple Mountain Landscape, 1953 (fig. 13)
Watercolor, 22 x 30 inches (54.8 x 76.2 cm); Private Collection

Milton Avery
Pale Field, Dark Mountain, 1959 (fig. 14)
Oil on canvas, 40 x 54 inches (101.6 x 137.2 cm); Collection of Mr. and Mrs. Heinz Eppler

Milton Avery
The Conversation, 1961 (fig. 15)
Oil on canvas, 28-1/2 x 37 inches (72.4 x 94 cm); Private Collection

Georg Baselitz, German, b. 1938
Stilleben, 1976-77 (fig. 46)
Acrylic on canvas, 98 x 78 inches (249 x 198.2 cm); Private Collection

William Baziotes, American, 1912-1963
Phantasm, 1951 (fig. 25)
Oil on canvas, 60 x 72 inches (152.4 x 170.2 cm); Collection of Mr. and Mrs. Heinz Eppler

Alexander Calder, American, 1898-1976
Through the Hoop, 1932 (fig. 11)
Pen and ink, 22 x 30 inches (54.8 x 76.2 cm); Collection of Mr. and Mrs. Heinz Eppler

Alexander Calder
Cantilever, 1940 (fig. 10)
Metal, 34 x 67 inches (86.4 x 170.2 cm); Private Collection

Alexander Calder
Calderoulette, 1940-45 (fig. 9)
Mixed media, H. 20-1/4 inches (51.5 cm); Collection of Mr. and Mrs. Heinz Eppler

Helen Frankenthaler, American, b. 1928
Red Support, 1964 (fig. 36)
Acrylic on canvas, 80 x 82 inches (203.2 x 208.3 cm); Collection of Mr. and Mrs. Edwin M. Roth

Helen Frankenthaler
The Big Dipper, 1985 (fig. 37)
Acrylic on canvas, 82 x 51-3/4 inches (208.3 x 131.5 cm); Private Collection

Arshile Gorky, American, b. Turkish Armenia, 1904-1948
Composition I, 1943 (fig. 16)
Pen, ink, and crayon, 18 x 24 inches (45.8 x 61 cm); Collection of Mr. and Mrs. Heinz Eppler

Adolph Gottlieb, American, 1903-1974
Brown Splash, 1970 (fig. 30)
Oil on canvas, 90 x 72 inches (228.6 x 182.9 cm); Collection of Mr. and Mrs. Heinz Eppler

Philip Guston, American, b. Canada, 1913-1980
Untitled, 1952 (fig. 32)
Oil on canvas, 32 x 35-7/8 inches (81.3 x 91.2 cm); Private Collection

Philip Guston
Entrance, 1979 (fig. 45)
Oil on canvas, 68 x 80 inches (172.7 x
203.3 cm); Private Collection

Al Held, American, b. 1928
Untitled No. 1, 1961 (fig. 42)
Acrylic on canvas, 84 x 60 inches (213.3 x
152.4 cm); Collection of Mr. and Mrs.
Frank H. Porter

David Hockney, British, b. 1937
Ann Reading, 1983 (fig. 49)
Charcoal on paper, 30 x 22-1/2 inches
(76.2 x 57.2 cm); Private Collection

Hans Hofmann, American, b. Germany,
1880-1966
Lava, 1960 (fig. 12)
Oil on canvas, 72 x 60 inches (182.9 x
152.4 cm); Collection of Mr. and Mrs.
Heinz Eppler

Ellsworth Kelly, American, b. 1923
Blue Red, 1965 (fig. 43)
Oil on canvas, 65 x 150 inches (165.1 x
381 cm); Collection of Mr. and Mrs. Frank
H. Porter

Tony King, American, b. 1944
Untitled, 1979 (fig. 44)
Acrylic on canvas, 68 x 68 inches (172.7 x
172.7 cm); Collection of Mr. and Mrs.
Edwin M. Roth

R. B. Kitaj, American, b. 1923
Starting a War, 1980-81 (fig. 48)
Oil on canvas, 84 x 36 inches (213.3 x
91.4 cm); Private Collection

Franz Kline, American, 1910-1962
Untitled, ca. 1958 (fig. 22)
Oil on paper, 12-1/2 x 10 inches (31.7 x
25.3 cm); Private Collection

Franz Kline
Light Mechanic, 1960 (fig. 23)
Oil on canvas, 92 x 67-1/2 inches
(233.7 x 171.5 cm); Collection of Mr.
and Mrs. Heinz Eppler

Willem de Kooning, American, b. Holland,
1904
Composition I, 1955 (fig. 17)
Oil on board, 23 x 22-3/4 inches (58.4 x
57.8 cm); Collection of Mr. and Mrs.
Heinz Eppler

Willem de Kooning
Untitled, 1976 (fig. 18)
Oil and newsprint mounted on canvas, 22
x 29 inches (54.8 x 73.7 cm);
Private Collection

Willem de Kooning
Untitled XV, 1977 (fig. 19)
Oil on canvas, 55 x 59 inches (139.7 x
149.8 cm); Private Collection

Fernand Léger, French, 1881-1955
La Grande Parade, 1953 (fig. 6)
Pen and ink, 21 x 26 inches (53.3 x 66
cm); Collection of Mr. and Mrs. Heinz
Eppler

Alfred Leslie, American, b. 1927
Instant Pictures, 1981 (fig. 50)
Oil on canvas, 84 x 60 inches (213.4 x
152.4 cm); Private Collection

Agnes Martin, American, b. Canada, 1912
The City, 1966 (fig. 40)
Acrylic on canvas, 72 x 72 inches (182.9 x
182.9 cm); Private Collection

Henri Matisse, French, 1869-1954
Nu Reflété dans la Glace, 1936 (fig. 4)
Pen and ink, 20 x 15 inches (50.8 x 38.1
cm); Collection of Mr. and Mrs. Heinz
Eppler

Joan Miró, Spanish, 1893-1983
La Revue, 1954 (fig. 8)
Gouache on paper, 16 x 25 inches (40.7 x
63.5 cm); Collection of Mr. and Mrs. Heinz
Eppler

Joan Mitchell, American, b. 1926
Untitled No. 3, 1953-54 (fig. 21)
Oil on canvas, 69 x 65 inches (175.3 x
165.1 cm); Collection of Mr. and Mrs.
Edwin M. Roth

Laszlo Moholy-Nagy, Hungarian,
1895-1946
Chicago February II, 1943 (fig. 7)
Oil on canvas, 30 x 39 inches (76.2 x 99.1
cm); Collection of Mr. and Mrs. Frank H.
Porter

Robert Motherwell, American, b. 1915
Je T'Aime, 1955 (fig. 26)
Oil on canvas, 72 x 54 inches (182.9 x
137.2 cm); Collection of Mr. and Mrs.
Heinz Eppler

Robert Motherwell
M, 1974 (fig. 27)
Collage, 72 x 36 inches (182.9 x 91.4 cm);
Private Collection

Robert Motherwell
Suchard, 1974 (fig. 28)
Collage and acrylic, 31 x 15-1/2 inches
(78.7 x 39.3 cm); Private Collection

Robert Motherwell
XYLOL, 1977 (fig. 29)
Collage on board, 36 x 24 inches (91.4 x
61 cm); Private Collection

Louise Nevelson, American, b. Russia,
1900
Floating Cloud Zag II, 1977 (fig. 41)
Painted wood, 42 x 50 x 7 inches (106.7 x
127 x 17.8 cm); Collection of Mr. and Mrs.
Heinz Eppler

Kenneth Noland, American, b. 1924
Warm Reverie, 1962 (fig. 34)
Acrylic on canvas, 45 x 45 inches (114.3 x
114.3 cm); Collection of Mr. and Mrs. Frank
H. Porter

Jules Olitski, American, b. Russia, 1922
The Abba's Palace, 1964 (fig. 35)
Acrylic on canvas, 92 x 72 inches (233.7 x
182.9 cm); Collection of Mr. and Mrs. Frank
H. Porter

Pablo Picasso, Spanish, 1881-1973
Baigneuse, 1908 (fig. 1)
Oil on canvas, 24 x 18 inches (61 x 45.8
cm); Collection of Mr. and Mrs. Frank H.
Porter

Pablo Picasso
Napolitaine à Poisson, 1919 (fig. 2)
Pen and ink, 12 x 8 inches (30.5 x 20.3
cm); Collection of Mr. and Mrs. Heinz
Eppler

Pablo Picasso
Portrait de Femme, 1943 (fig. 3)
Oil on canvas, 29 x 24 inches (73.7 x 61
cm); Collection of Mr. and Mrs. Heinz
Eppler

Mark Rothko, American, b. Russia,
1903-1970
Orange, Red, Yellow, 1956 (fig. 24)
Oil on canvas, 79 x 69 inches (200.6 x
175.3 cm); Collection of Mr. and Mrs.
Heinz Eppler

Georges Rouault, French, 1871-1958
Paysage Biblique (fig. 5)
Oil on canvas, 16-1/8 x 20-1/2 inches
(41 x 52 cm); Collection of Mr. and Mrs.
Edwin M. Roth

Morteza Sazegar, American, b. Iran, 1933
C7-71, 1971 (fig. 38)
Acrylic on canvas, 80 x 50-1/2 inches
(203.2 x 128.3 cm); Collection of Mr. and
Mrs. Frank H. Porter

David Smith, American, 1906-1965
Volton XXIV, 1963 (fig. 31)
Steel, 98 x 33 x 13 inches (249 x 83.8 x 33
cm); Collection of Mr. and Mrs. Heinz
Eppler

Frank Stella, American, b. 1936
Slieve More, 1964 (fig. 39)
Acrylic on canvas, 77 x 81-1/2 inches
(167.6 x 207 cm); Private Collection

Antonio Tapies, Spanish, b. 1923
No. 10F, 1964 (fig. 33)
Oil and collage on canvas, 66 x 77 inches
(167.6 x 195.6 cm); Collection of Mr. and
Mrs. Frank H. Porter

Jack Tworkov, American, b. Poland, 1900
Simile of the Crab, 1962 (fig. 20)
Oil on canvas, 90-1/2 x 40-1/2 inches
(229.9 x 102.8 cm); Private Collection

Catalogue

The first few decades of the twentieth century were crucial years in the development of modern art. Extending the experiments of the Post-Impressionists Paul Cézanne, Georges Seurat, Vincent van Gogh, and Paul Gauguin, artists such as Pablo Picasso (figs. 1-3), Fernand Léger (fig. 6), Henri Matisse (fig. 4), and Georges Rouault (fig. 5) created the key movements of Cubism, Fauvism, and [French] Expressionism.

All of these new movements emphasized form but retained recognizable subject matter. Fauvism and Expressionism distorted images and color for decorative purposes and to indicate emotional content. Cubism, on the other hand, co-invented by Picasso and Braque, repressed color and emotion to concentrate on a structural conception of objects and the integration of matter and space. Picasso's *Bather* (fig. 1) is an example of early Analytical Cubism, wherein figures and objects are rendered in terms of small planes derived from an analysis of the entire structure of a form rather than as seen from a single, fixed viewpoint.

Even though Cubist artists evolved individual styles, most of them remained within a consistent stylistic tradition. Only Picasso constantly created new means of expression, as the lovely classical drawing of a woman holding a fish (fig. 2) and the later Cubist-Expressionist portrait of a woman (fig. 3) attest. Léger's complex black and white drawing (fig. 6) reveals an unusual development of tightly integrated Cubist composition in this artist's sturdy hands. Rouault's *Paysage Biblique* (fig. 5) is a typical deep-toned, mysterious, peopled-landscape by a Fauve painter who developed a French version of Expressionism, whereas Matisse's lovely drawing *Nu Reflété dans la Glace* (fig. 4) demonstrates how this leader of the Fauve movement—like the Renaissance artist Sandro Botticelli—evolved a poignantly decorative style that raised decoration to the highest aesthetic level.

Cubism was carried into complete abstraction by artists such as Wassily Kandinsky, Robert Delaunay, and Piet Mondrian. Working in the same idiom, Hungarian constructivist Laszlo Moholy-Nagy created compelling geometrical paintings, such as *Chicago February II* (fig. 7), that are meticulously drawn and composed.

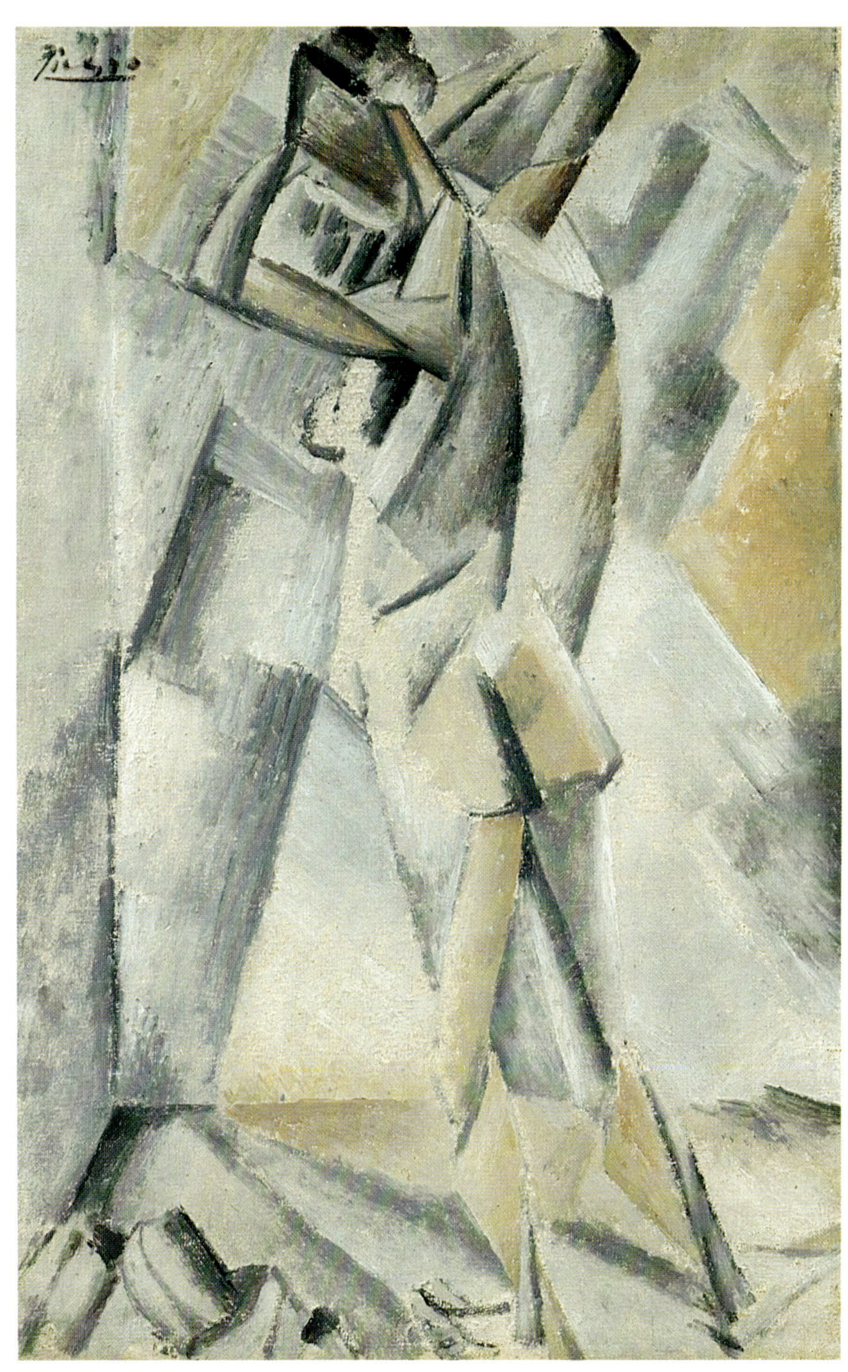

1. Pablo Picasso
Baigneuse (*Bather*), 1908,
oil on canvas.

2. Pablo Picasso
Napolitaine à Poisson
(*Neapolitan Woman with*
Fish), 1919, pen and ink.

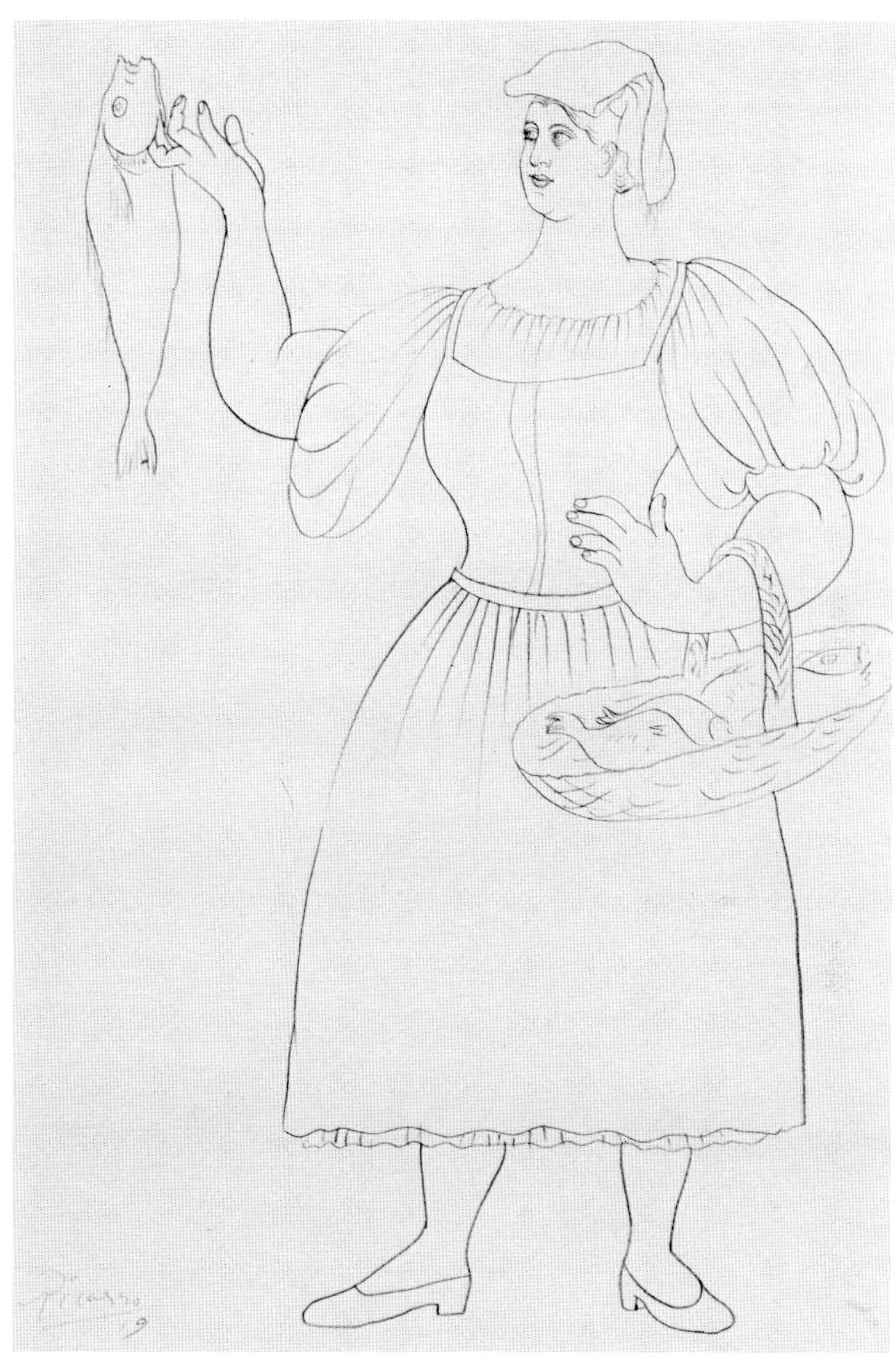

3. Pablo Picasso
Portrait de Femme (*Portrait of a Woman*), 1943, oil on canvas.

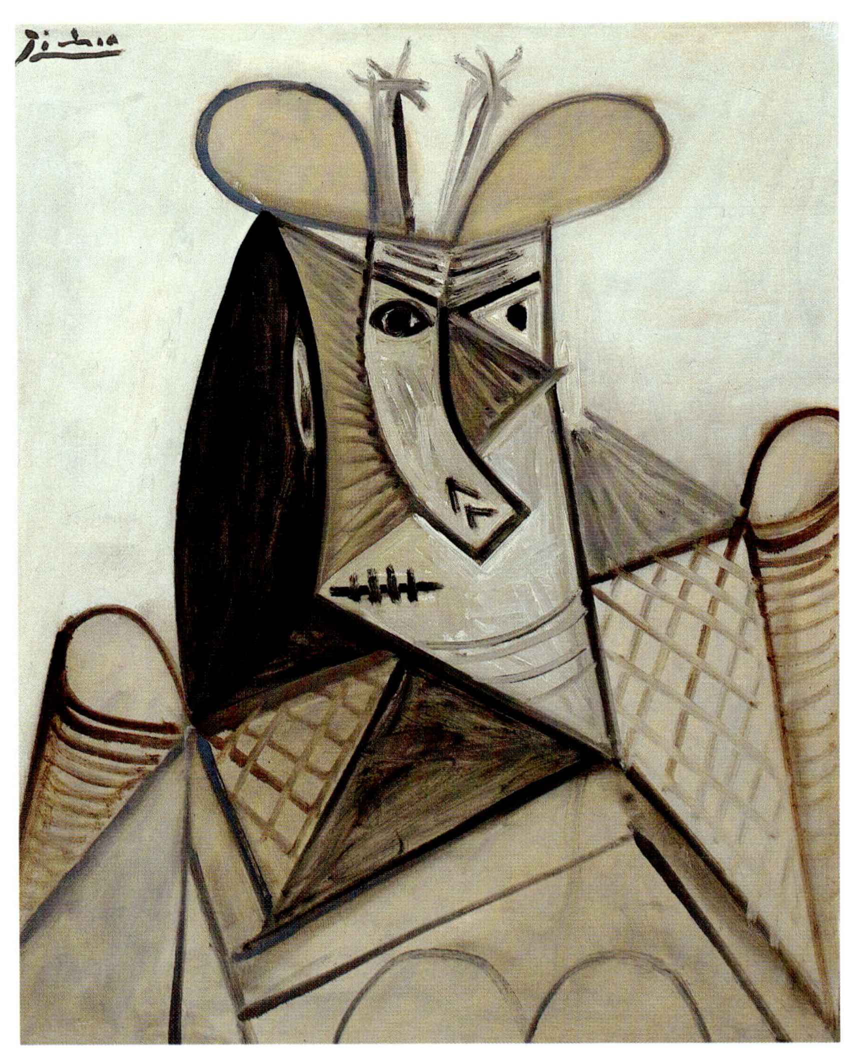

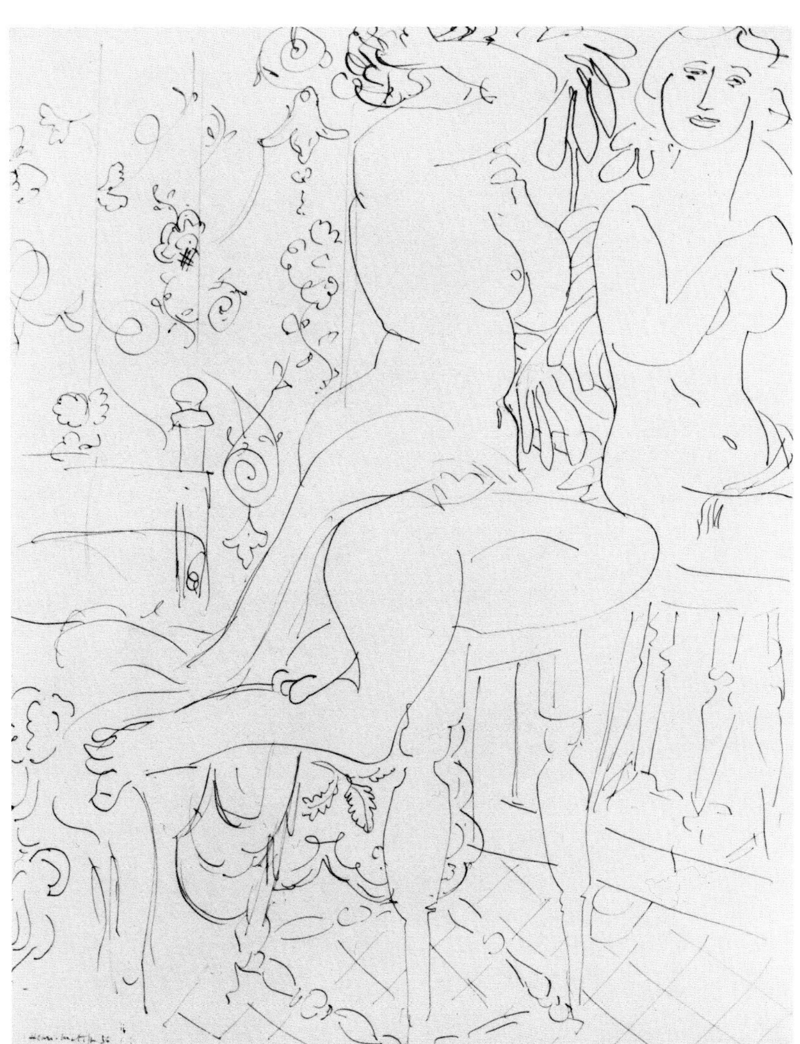

5. Georges Rouault
Paysage Biblique (*Biblical
Landscape*), oil on canvas.

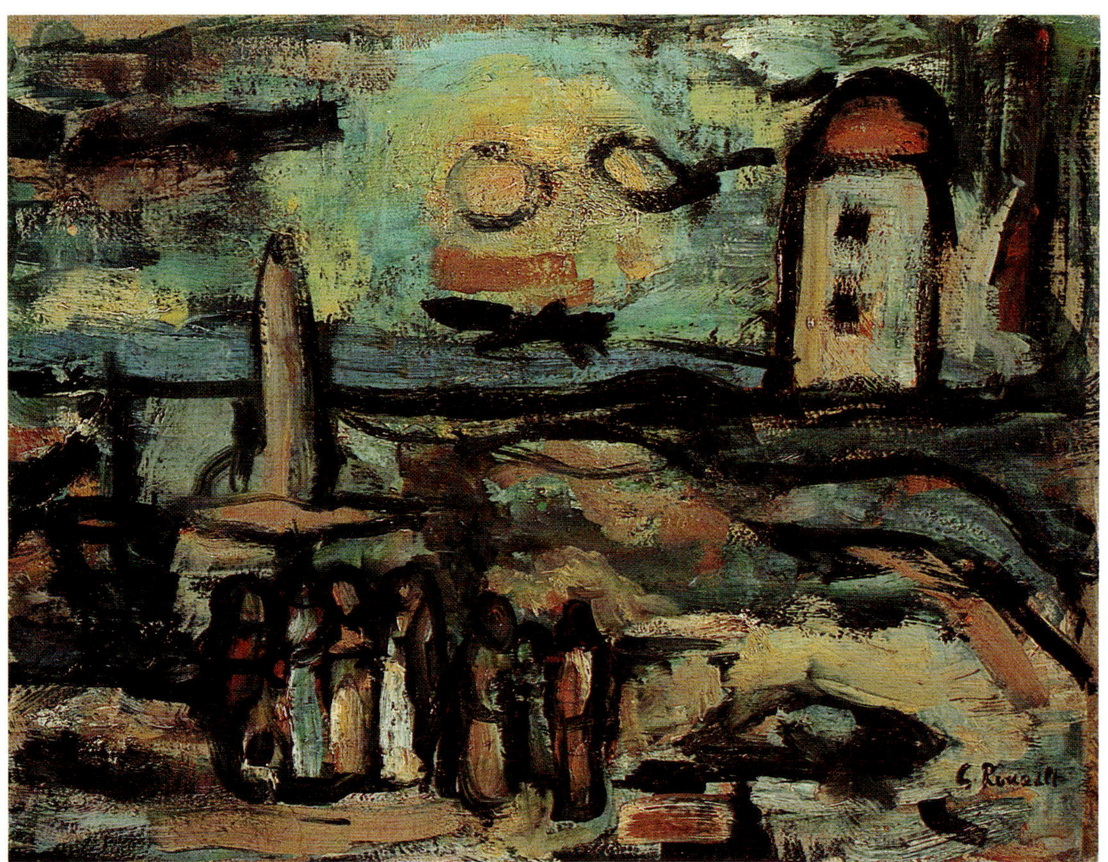

6. Fernand Léger
La Grande Parade (*The Big Parade*), 1953, pen and ink.

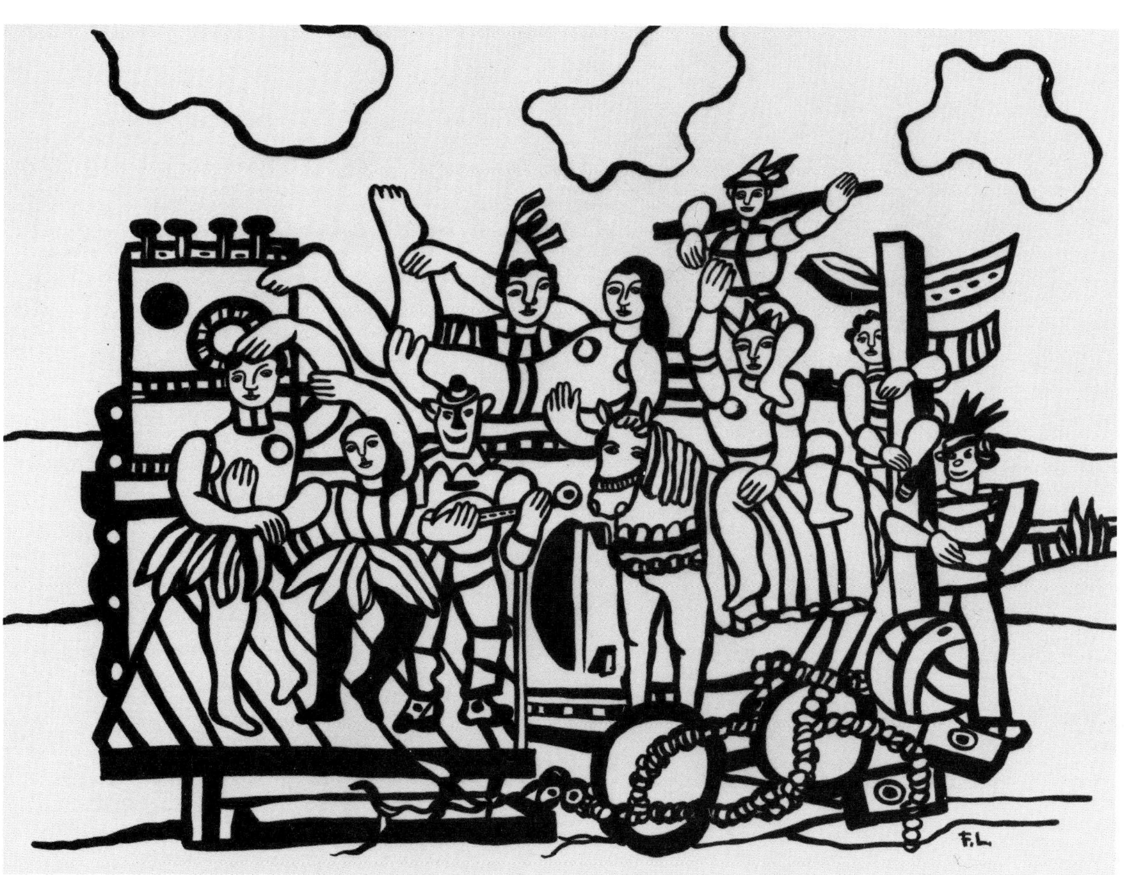

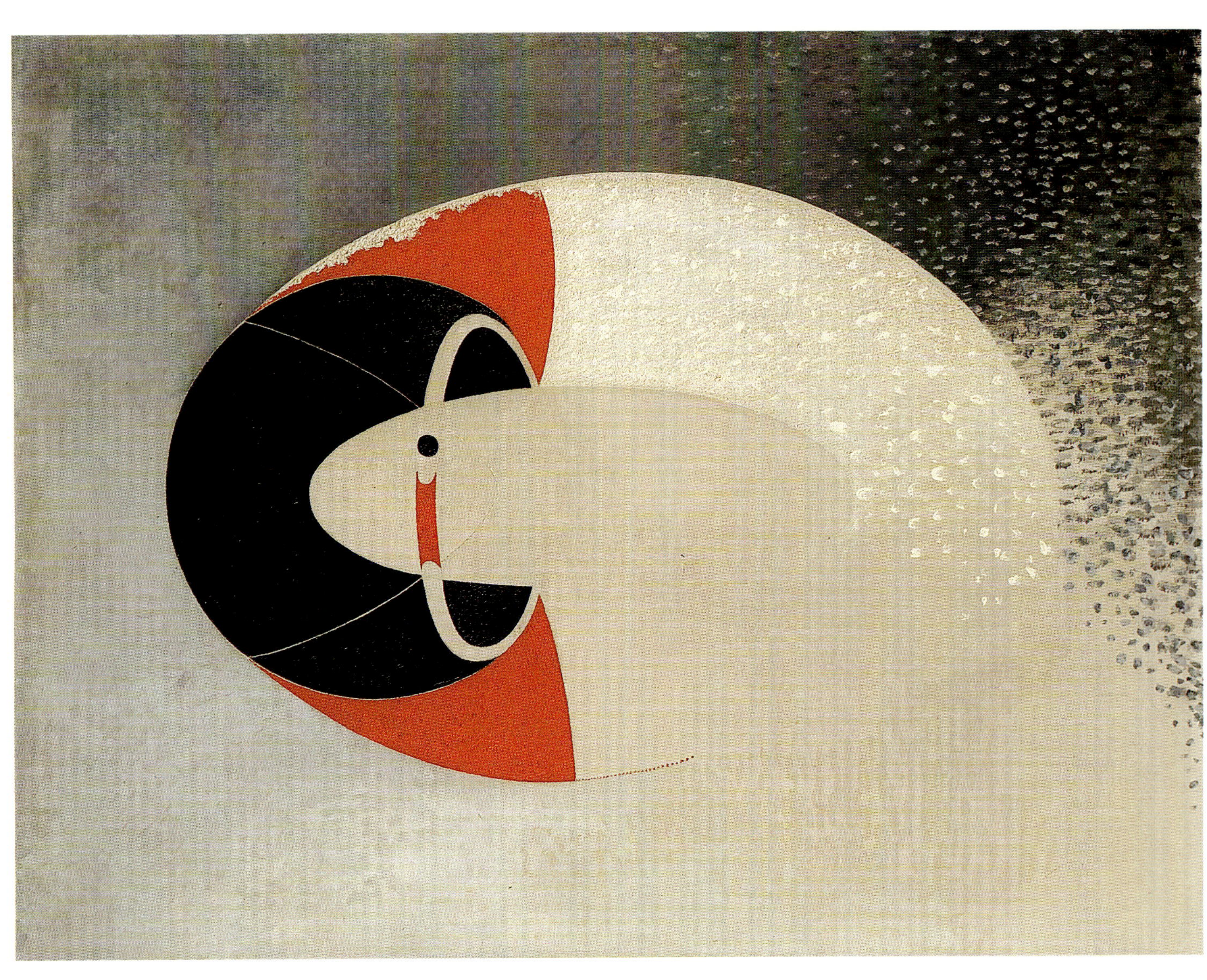

In the mid-twenties Surrealism developed as a reaction against the extreme formalism of Cubism and abstract art. Accepting Sigmund Freud's ''unconscious'' as a new source for subject matter, the Surrealists used dreams and automatic drawing and painting as a means to release images from the control of the conscious mind.

The Spanish painter Joan Miró, one of the original members of the Surrealist movement, did the colorful gouache painting *La Revue* (fig. 8) as one of a set of illustrations for Alfred Jarry's bizarre play *Ubu Roi*.

Alexander Calder, a fringe member of the Surrealist movement, was influenced by Miró but was even more playful in spirit. Two of his early sculptures, *Calderoulette* (fig. 9) and *Cantilever* (fig. 10), as well as the even earlier drawing *Through the Hoop* (fig. 11), all demonstrate the buoyant wit that infuses Calder's work.

8. Joan Miró
La Revue (The Revue),
1954, gouache on paper.

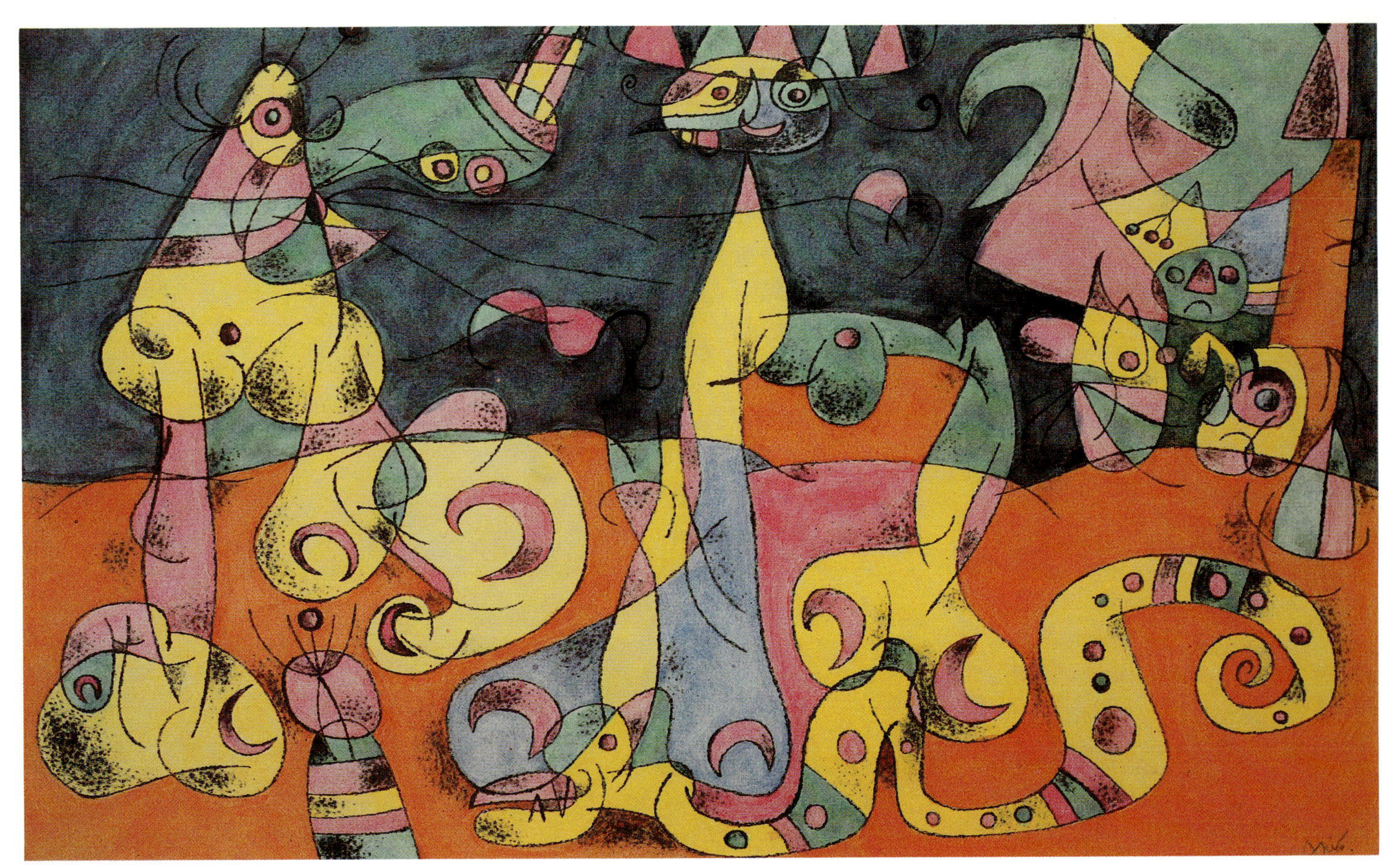

9. Alexander Calder
Calderoulette, 1940-45,
mixed media.

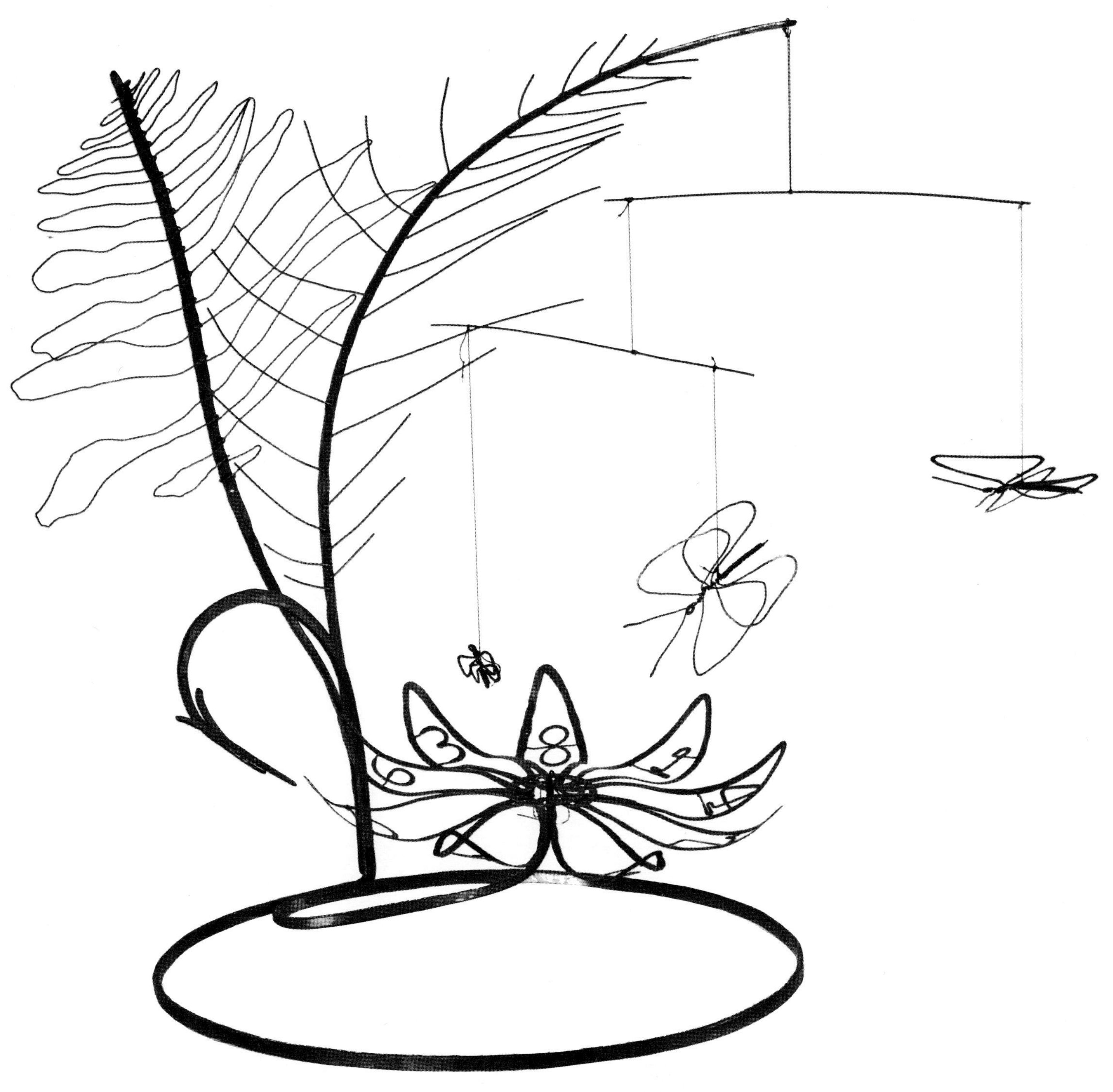

10. Alexander Calder
Cantilever, 1940, metal.

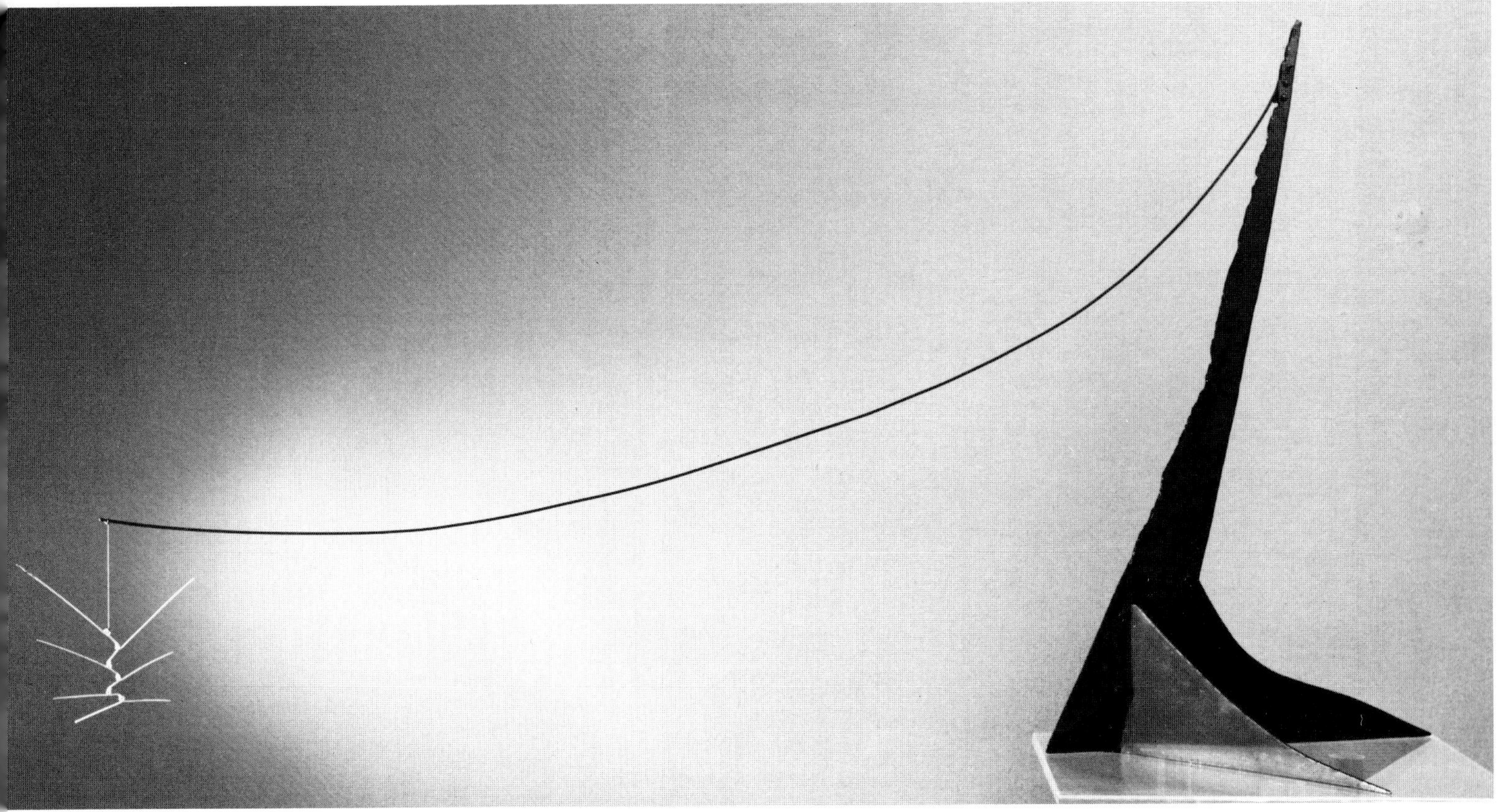

11. Alexander Calder
Through the Hoop, 1932,
pen and ink.

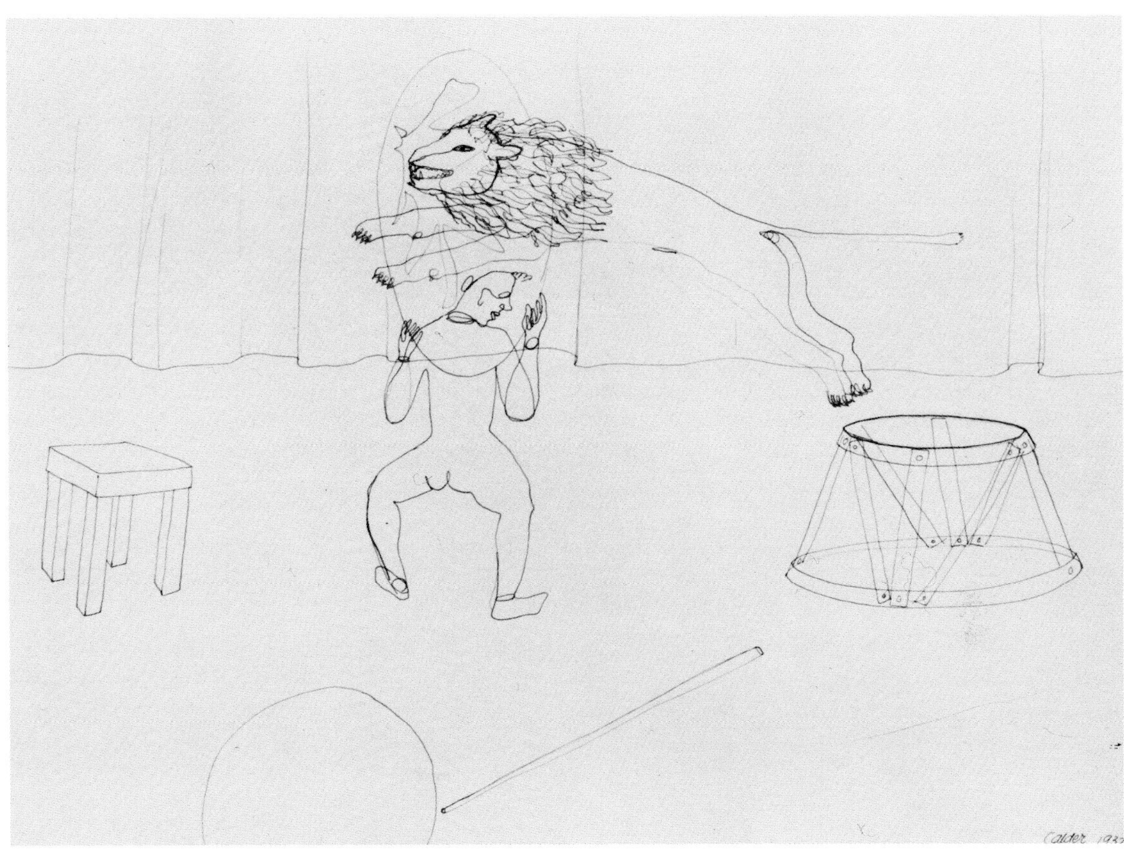

During the war years of 1939 to 1945, a remarkable development in painting occurred in and around New York City that has variously been called: ''the New York School,'' ''Action Painting,'' and ''Abstract Expressionism.'' The abstract paintings and drawings by artists belonging to this group evolved directly out of the act of painting rather than from prior mental models. Their works functioned as visual metaphors of their own feelings and thoughts stimulated during the act of creating.

While Surrealism provided an initial impetus for this movement, some other influences were: Hans Hofmann, a German-refugee painter and teacher; Milton Avery, an older American painter who had earlier been influenced by Matisse; and Arshile Gorky, an Armenian-born contemporary of the Abstract Expressionists.

Hofmann's richly colored, thickly painted canvas *Lava* (fig. 12) demonstrates his great ability to suggest conflicting movements in space and, at the same time, to develop a cohesive surface composition. Milton Avery's thinly painted compositions, such as *Purple Mountain Landscape* (fig. 13), *Pale Field, Dark Mountain* (fig. 14), and *The Conversation* (fig. 15), dispose broad areas of rich color—evidence of his debt to Matisse, on the one hand, and his influence on Rothko on the other. Gorky's dense, brilliantly colored drawing *Composition I* (fig. 16) illustrates his masterful handling of shapes and colors that suggest figures in space.

12. Hans Hofmann
Lava, 1960, oil on canvas.

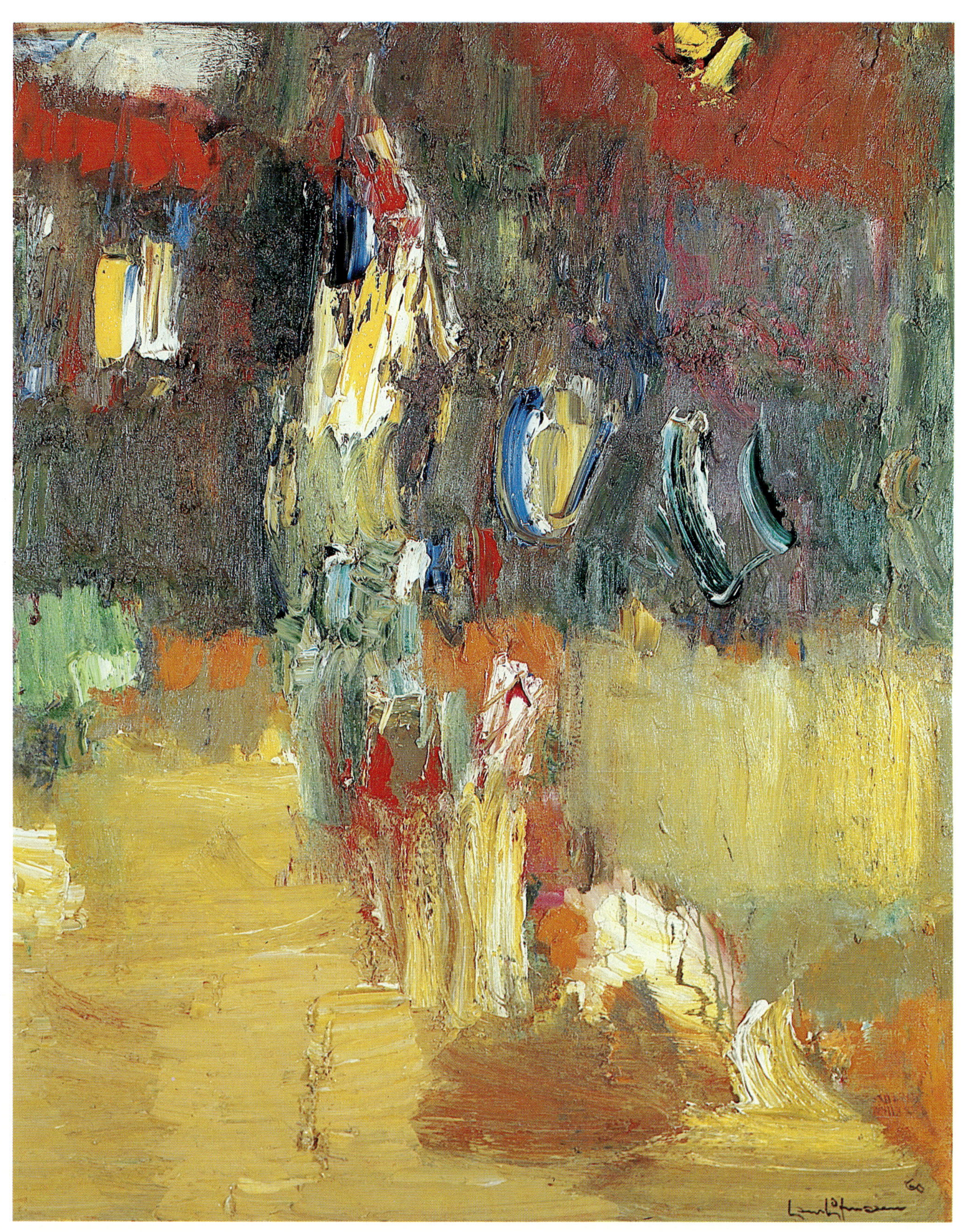

13. Milton Avery
Purple Mountain Land-
scape, 1953, watercolor.

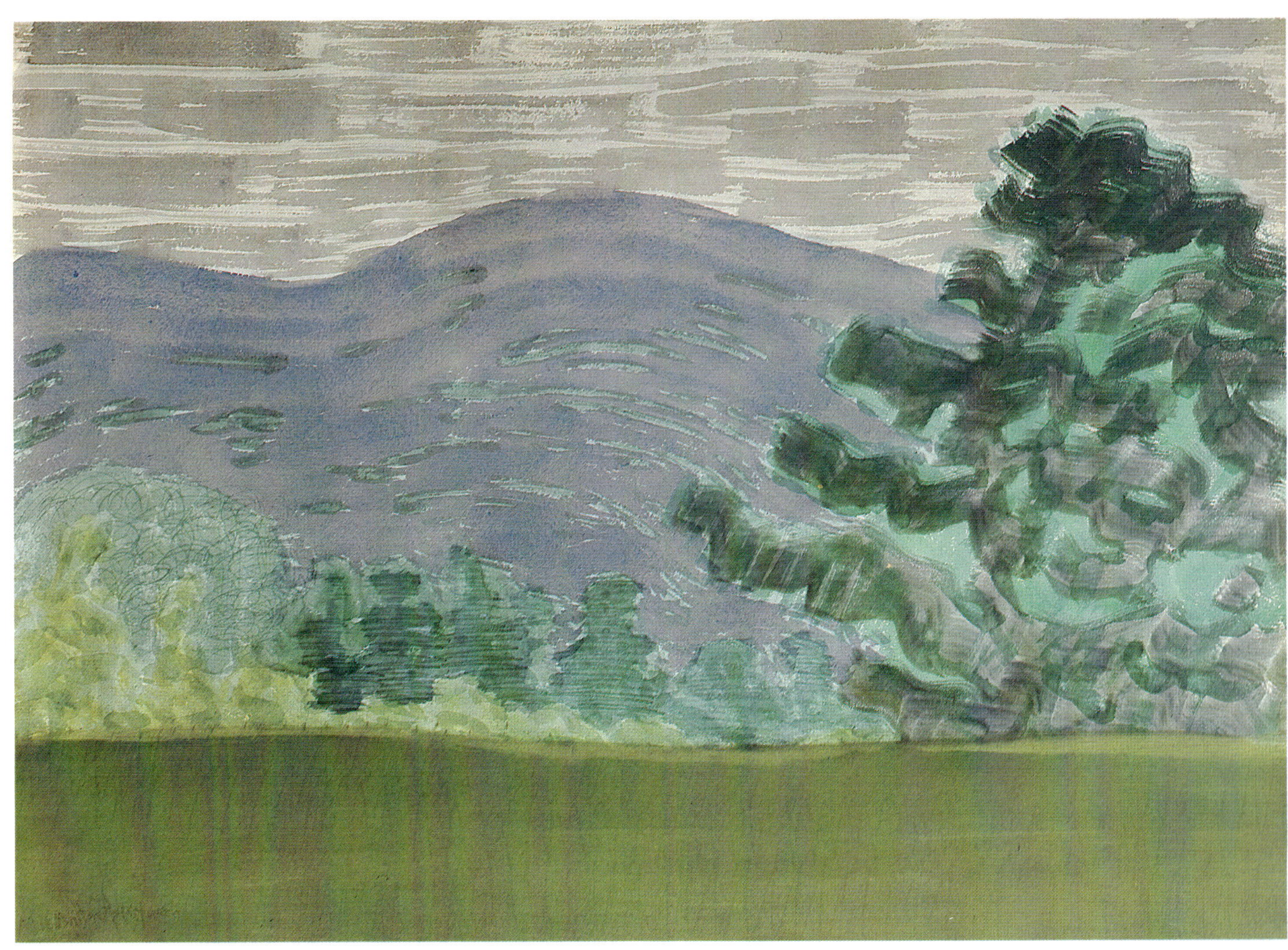

14. Milton Avery
Pale Field, Dark Mountain,
1959, oil on canvas.

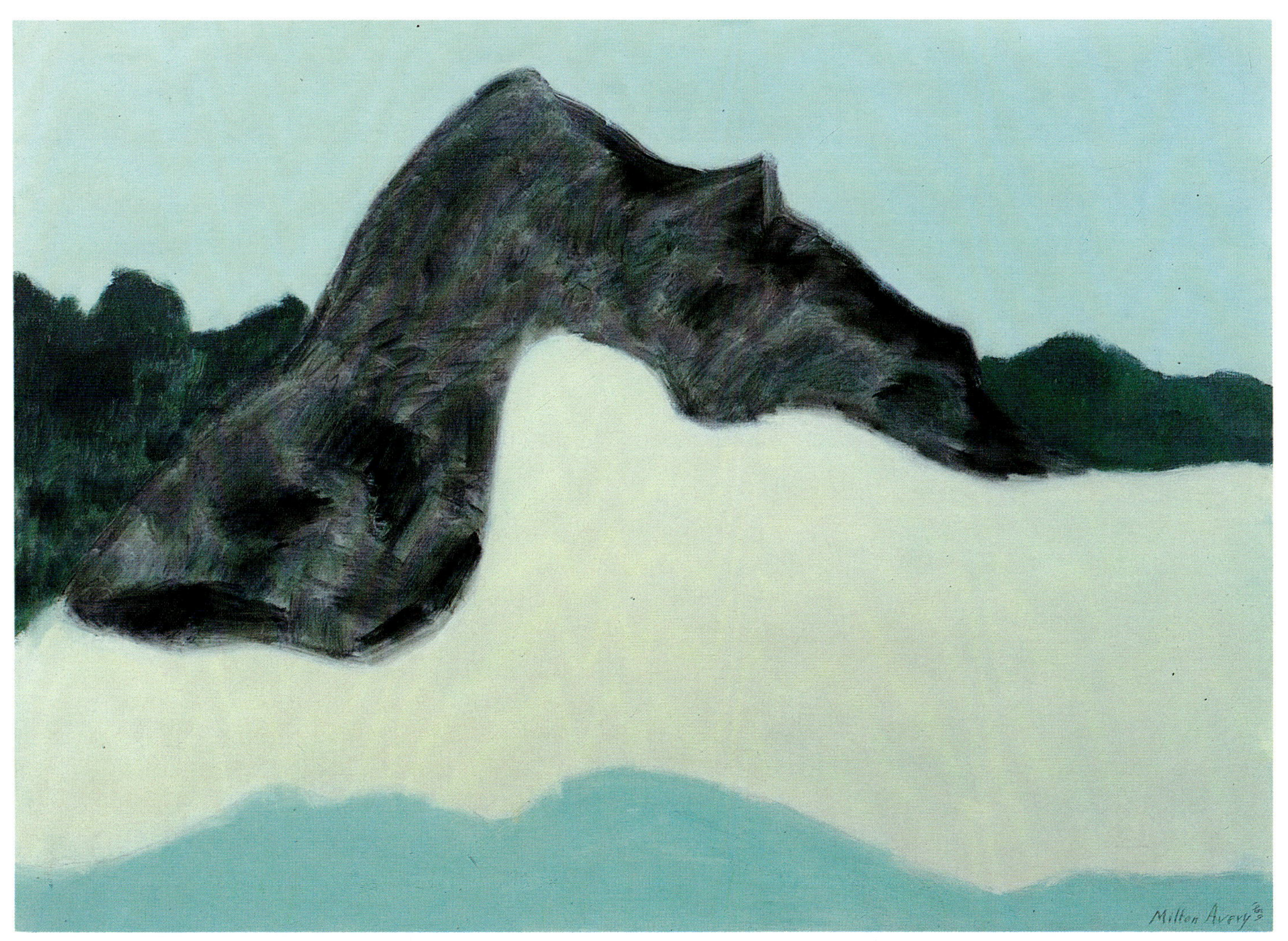

15. Milton Avery
The Conversation, 1961, oil
on canvas.

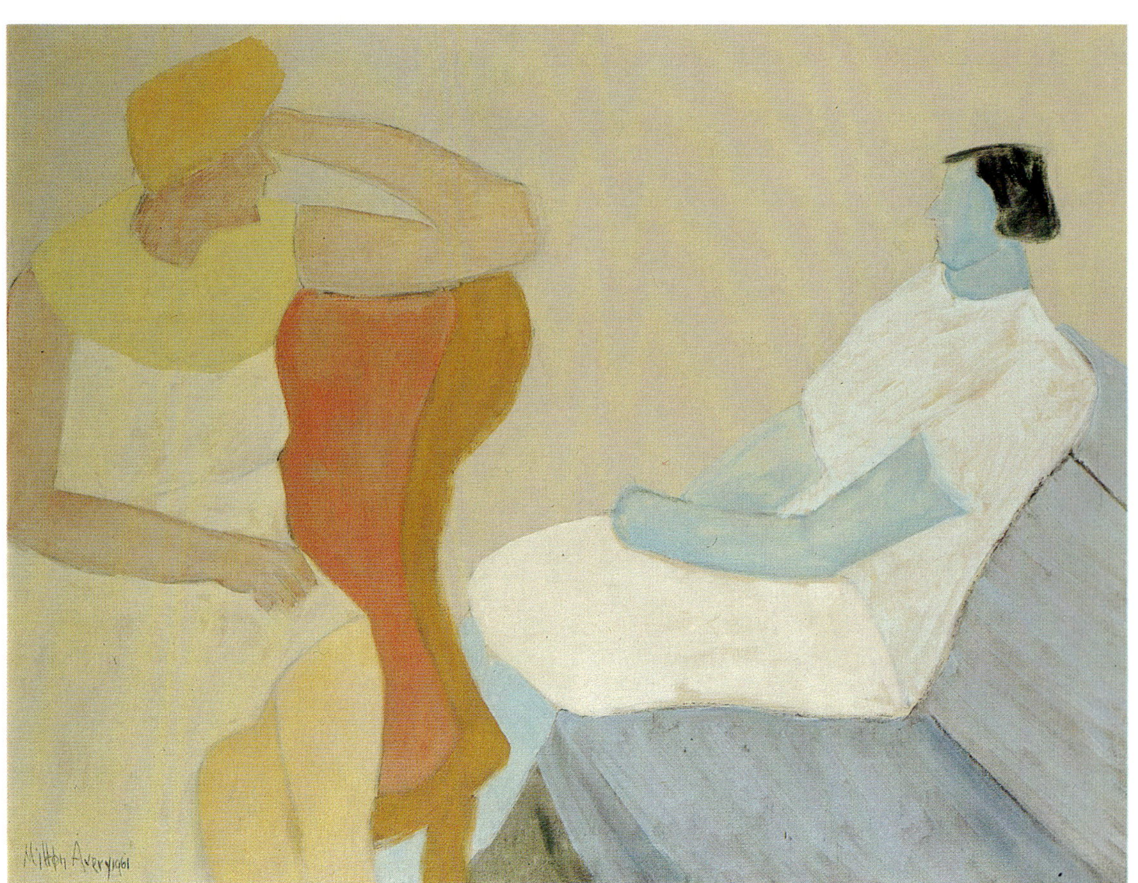

16. Arshile Gorky
Composition I, 1943, pen,
ink, and crayon.

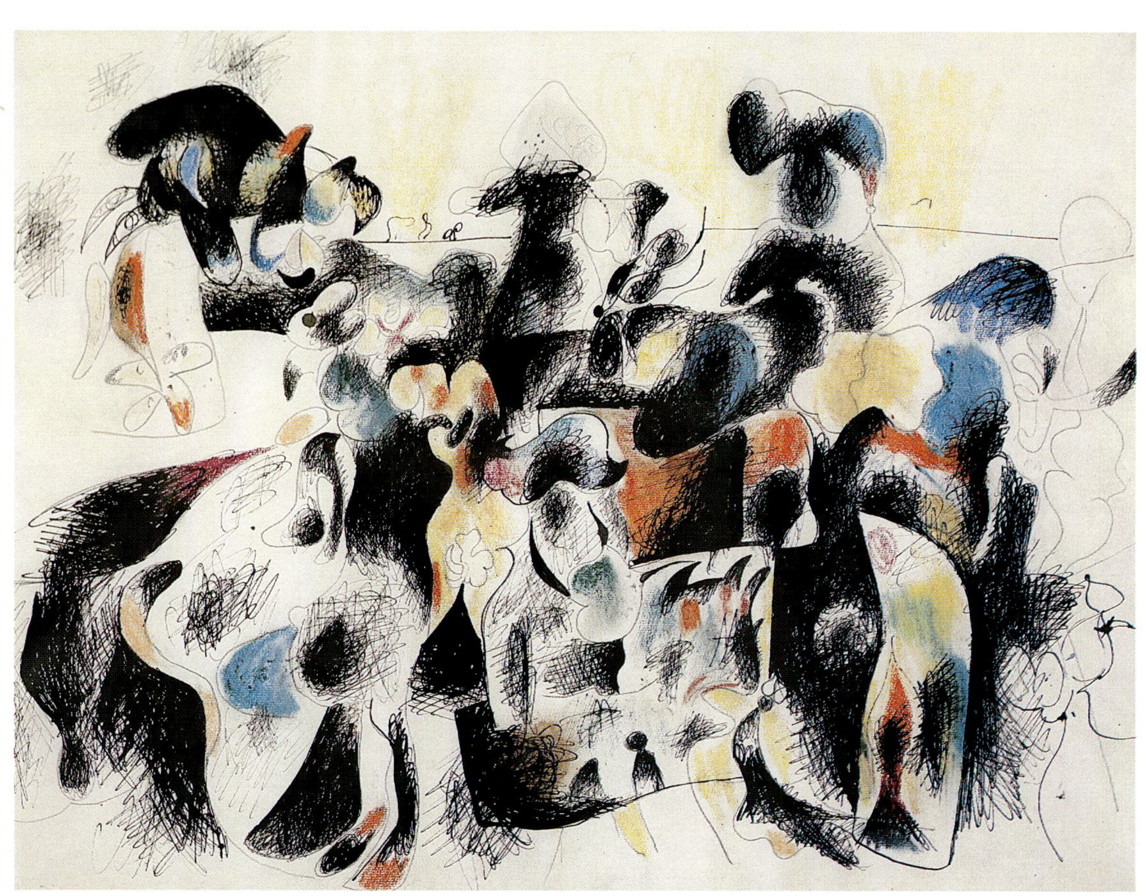

Stimulated by Surrealism and indebted to Cubism and earlier abstract art, Abstract Expressionism became the dominant art movement in the mid-forties to the mid-sixties. The movement was characterized by diverse personal styles.

Willem de Kooning, Jack Tworkov, and Joan Mitchell are best known for their ''gestural'' paintings done in the fifties and early sixties. Born and trained in Holland, de Kooning always retained some of the elegant character of European painting, as in *Composition I* (fig. 17), *Untitled* (fig. 18), and *Untitled XV* (fig. 19). Tworkov's *Simile of the Crab* (fig. 20), a fine example of his important work of the early sixties, integrates flamelike, diagonal strokes of color into loose, gridlike arrangements. Joan Mitchell belonged to the second generation of Abstract Expressionists, but her spontaneous, vibrant, linear style, exemplified in *Untitled No. 3* (fig. 21), is closely related to de Kooning and Tworkov.

Franz Kline began creating Abstract Expressionist paintings around 1950. His black and white paintings, such as *Light Mechanic* (fig. 23), and his untitled drawing (fig. 22) exhibit the vigorous energy and tension of New York City. Black bars drive across the surface of *Light Mechanic*, dividing the white ground into irregular, exciting shapes, but uniting the entire canvas into a single, dramatic image.

In contrast to the driving energy of Kline's paintings, Rothko's ambient, soft-edged, rectangular shapes hover silently one above the other—as in *Orange, Red, Yellow* (fig. 24); many layers of thin pigment create the impression of space and of a soft-hued, glowing atmosphere.

William Baziotes's work is close in spirit to Surrealism. In the late forties and early fifties his compositions, such as *Phantasm* (fig. 25), reveal strange, dreamlike worlds containing bizarre organic forms; deep blues, greens, and violets suggest a subterranean landscape.

Educated in philosophy and French literature, Robert Motherwell joined French elegance to American forthrightness in such collages as *M* (fig. 27), *Suchard* (fig. 28), and *XYLOL* (fig. 29), and paintings like *Je T'Aime* (fig. 26).

Adolph Gottlieb's paintings used flat shapes and spatial relationships rather than brushwork as primary expressive elements; his series generically titled ''Burst(s),'' including *Brown Splash* (fig. 30), typically relate a serene, cloudlike shape above to an explosive, linear shape below.

The preeminent American sculptor David Smith created large, welded-metal sculptures, such as *Volton XXIV* (fig. 31), that reveal his ability to combine delicate balance with raw power. He borrowed the technique of welding metal forms from Picasso and the Spanish sculptor Julio Gonzalez; however, the big, open spirit of Smith's sculpture distinguishes it from these Europeans and allies him with the Abstract Expressionist painters.

Philip Guston's style in the early fifties was labeled ''Abstract Impressionism'' to differentiate it from the more athletic works of Pollock, Kline, and de Kooning. Despite the sensuous, flickering brushwork of his paintings during this period, Guston's work clearly lies within the Abstract Expressionist tradition. In paintings such as *Untitled* (fig. 32), strokes overlap and interweave to create a shimmering tapestry of color that suggests light, space, and atmosphere.

The Spanish painter Antonio Tapies has produced some somber, earth-toned collages, like *No. 10F* (fig. 33), that parallel the grave spirit of works by many American Abstract Expressionists.

17. Willem de Kooning
Composition I, 1955, oil on
board.

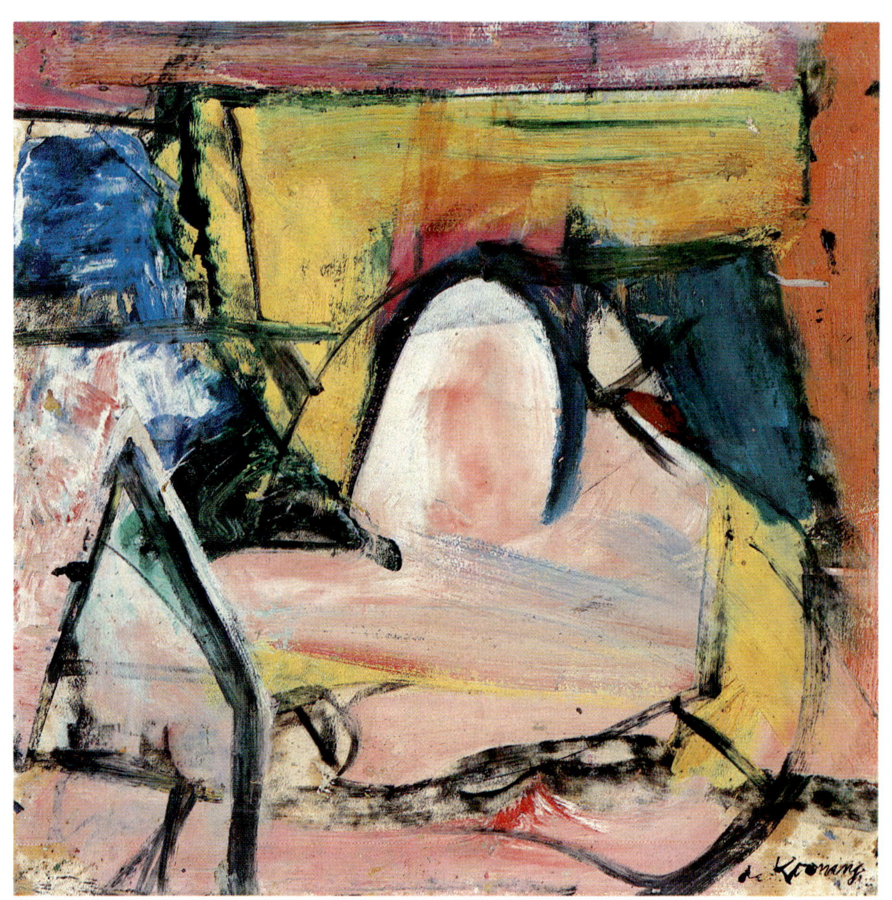

18. Willem de Kooning
Untitled, 1976, oil and
newsprint mounted on
canvas.

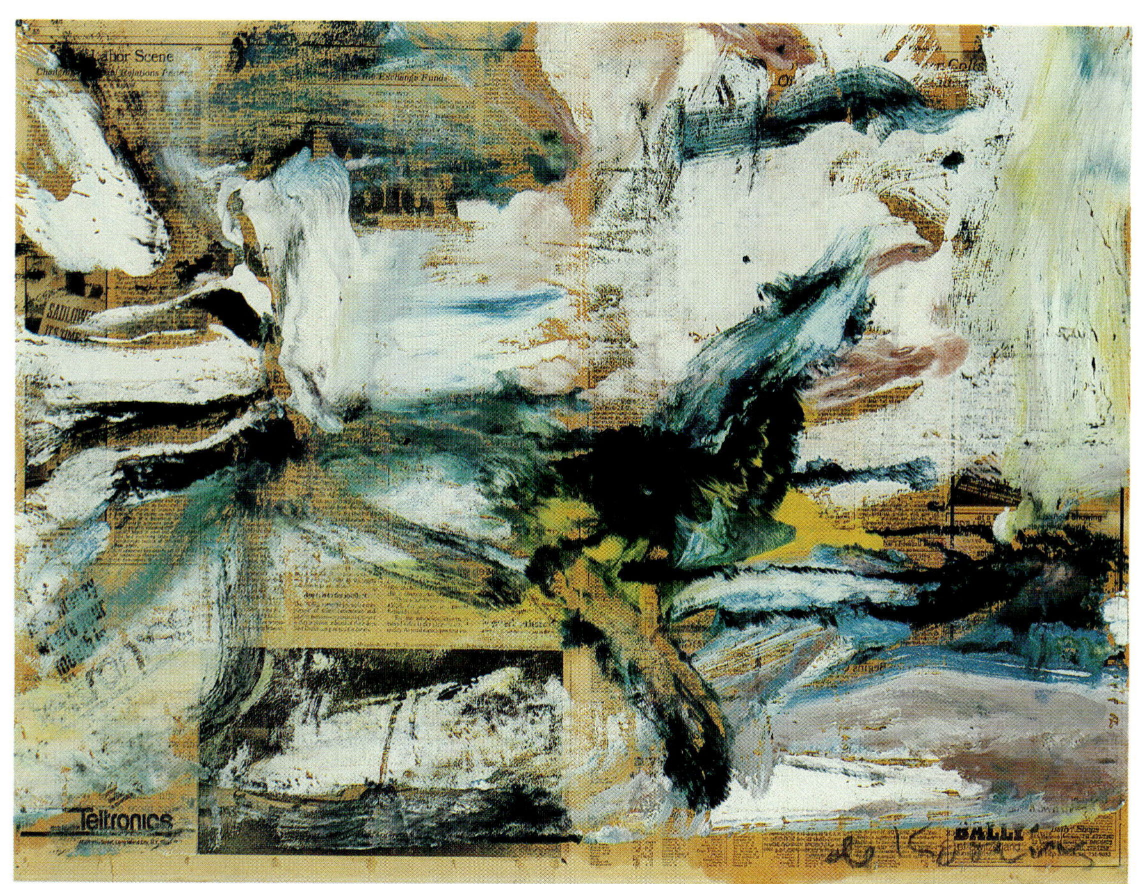

19. Willem de Kooning
Untitled XV, 1977, oil on
canvas.

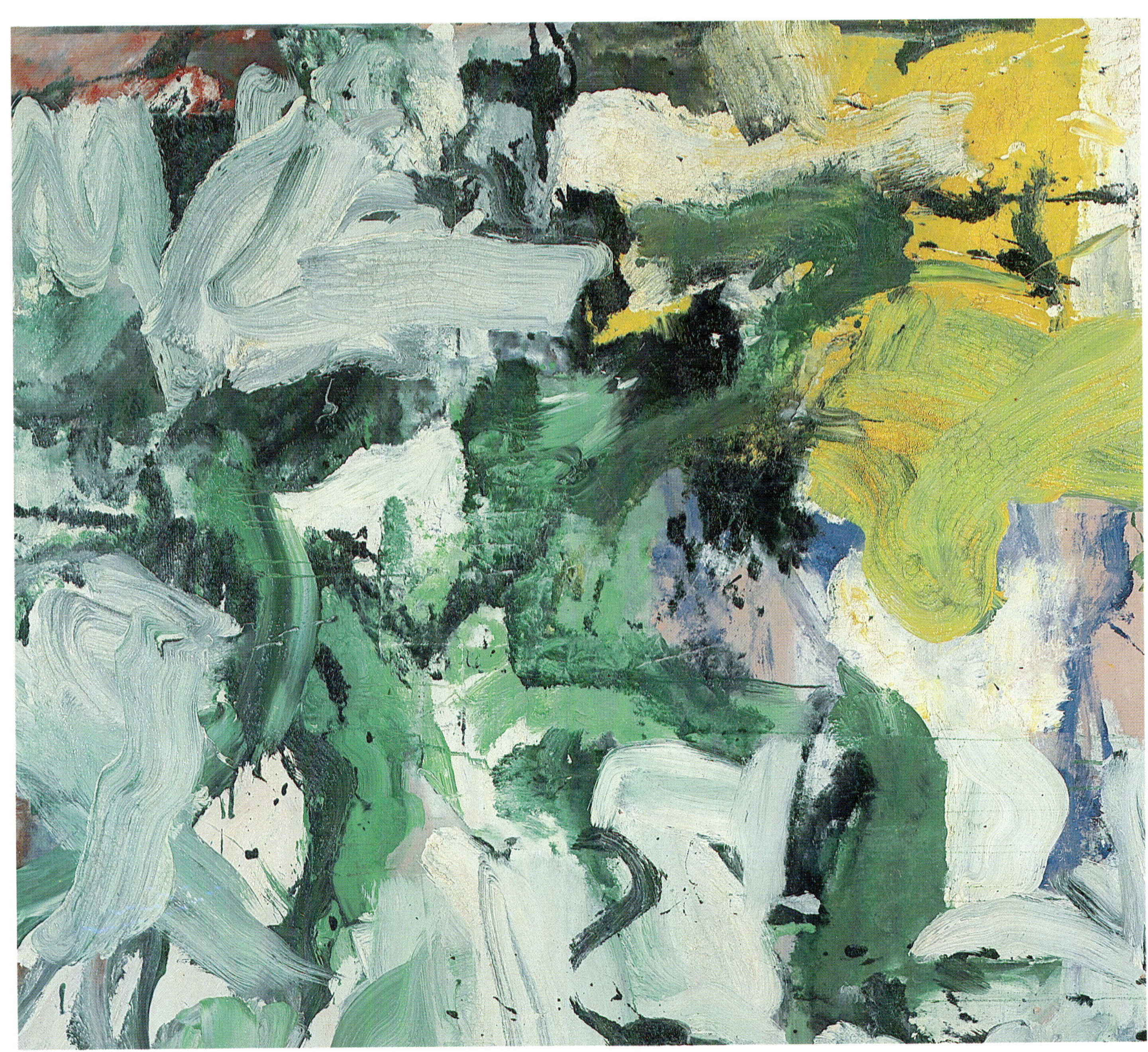

20. Jack Tworkov
Simile of the Crab, 1962, oil
on canvas.

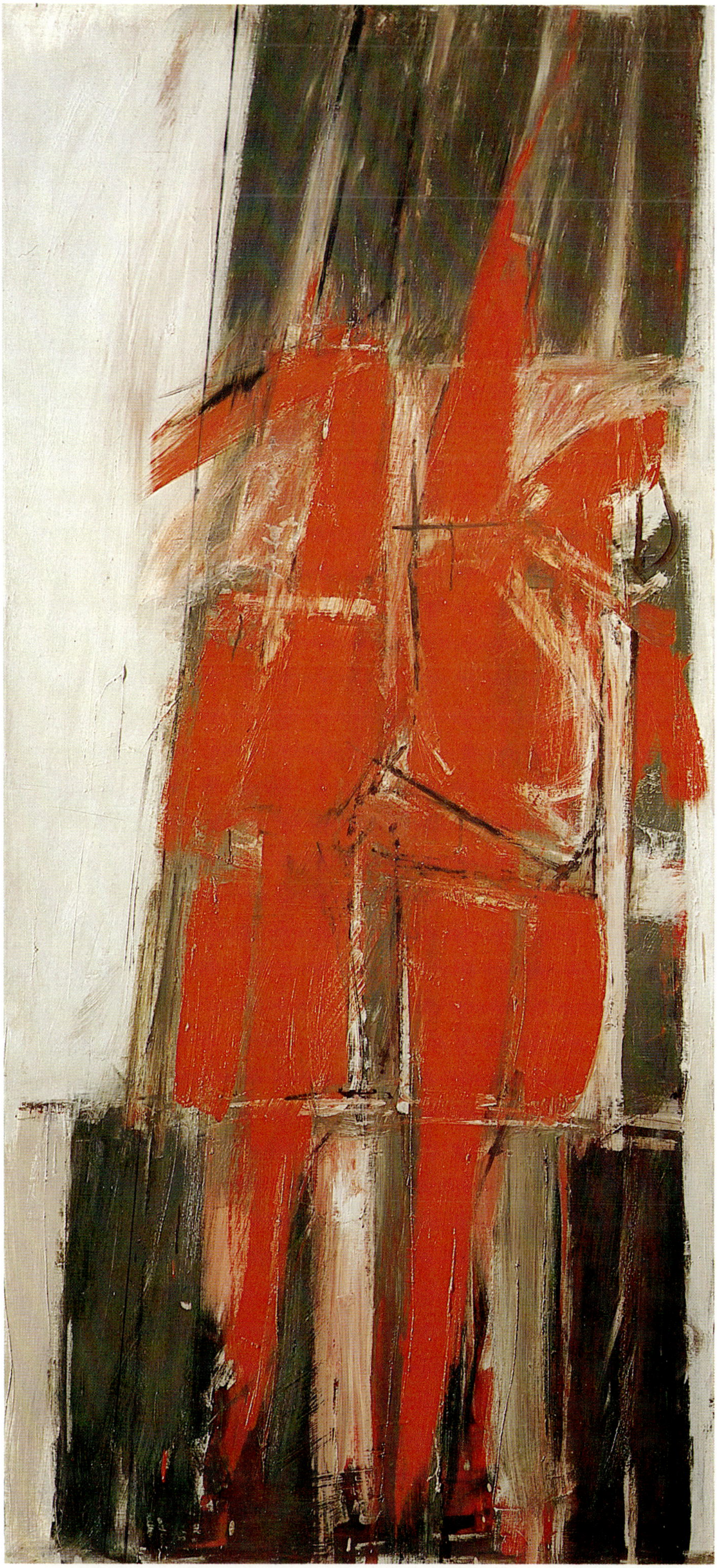

21. Joan Mitchell

Untitled No. 3, 1953-54, oil
on canvas.

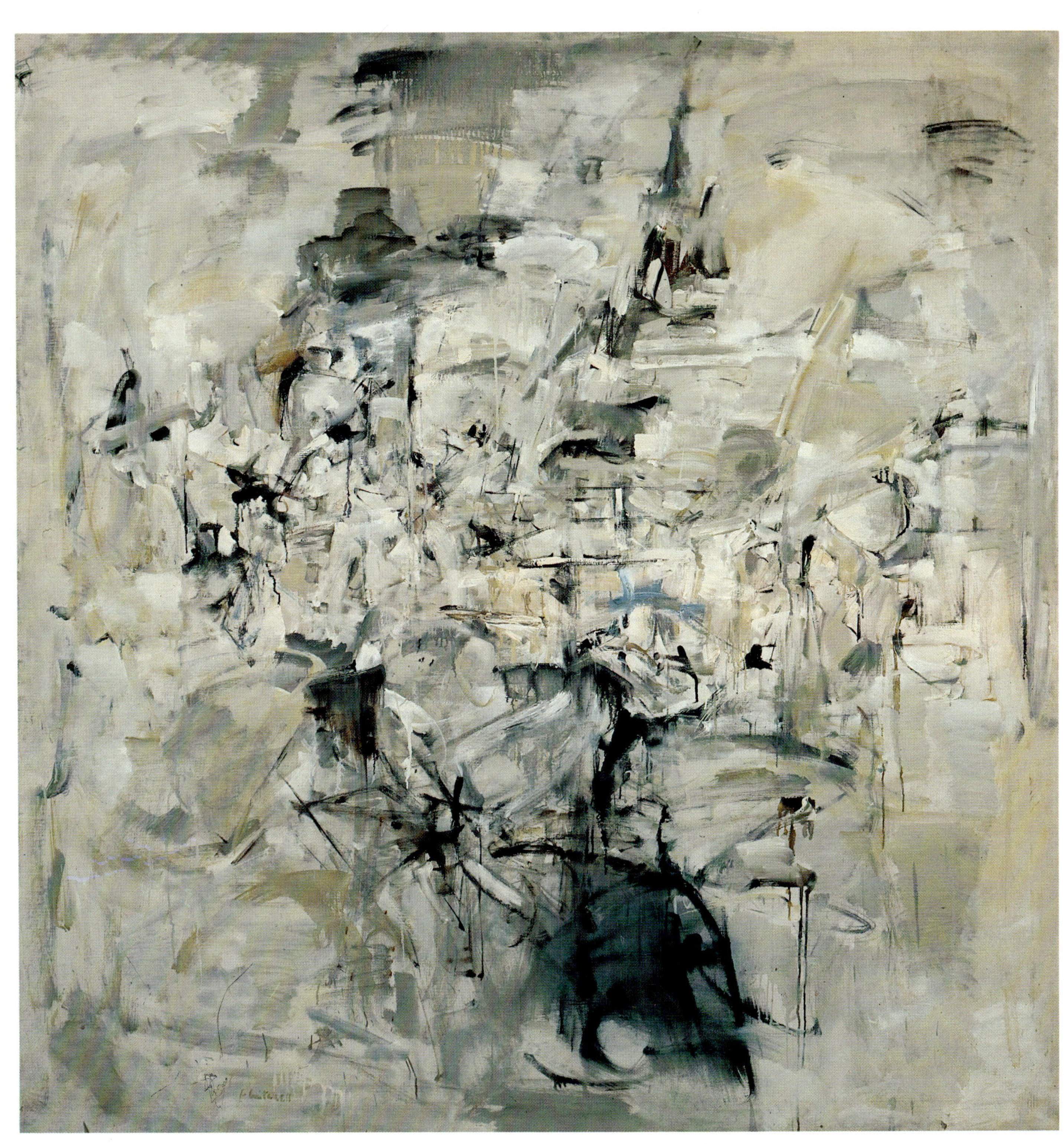

22. Franz Kline
Untitled, ca. 1958, oil on
paper.

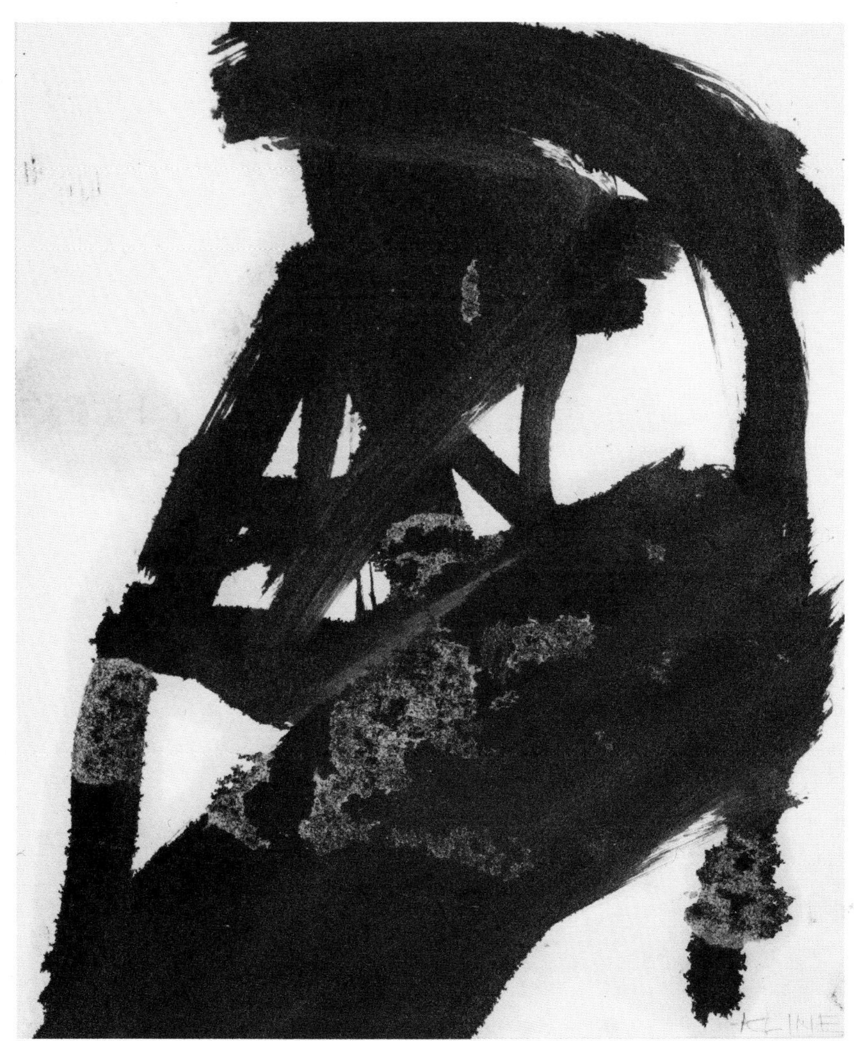

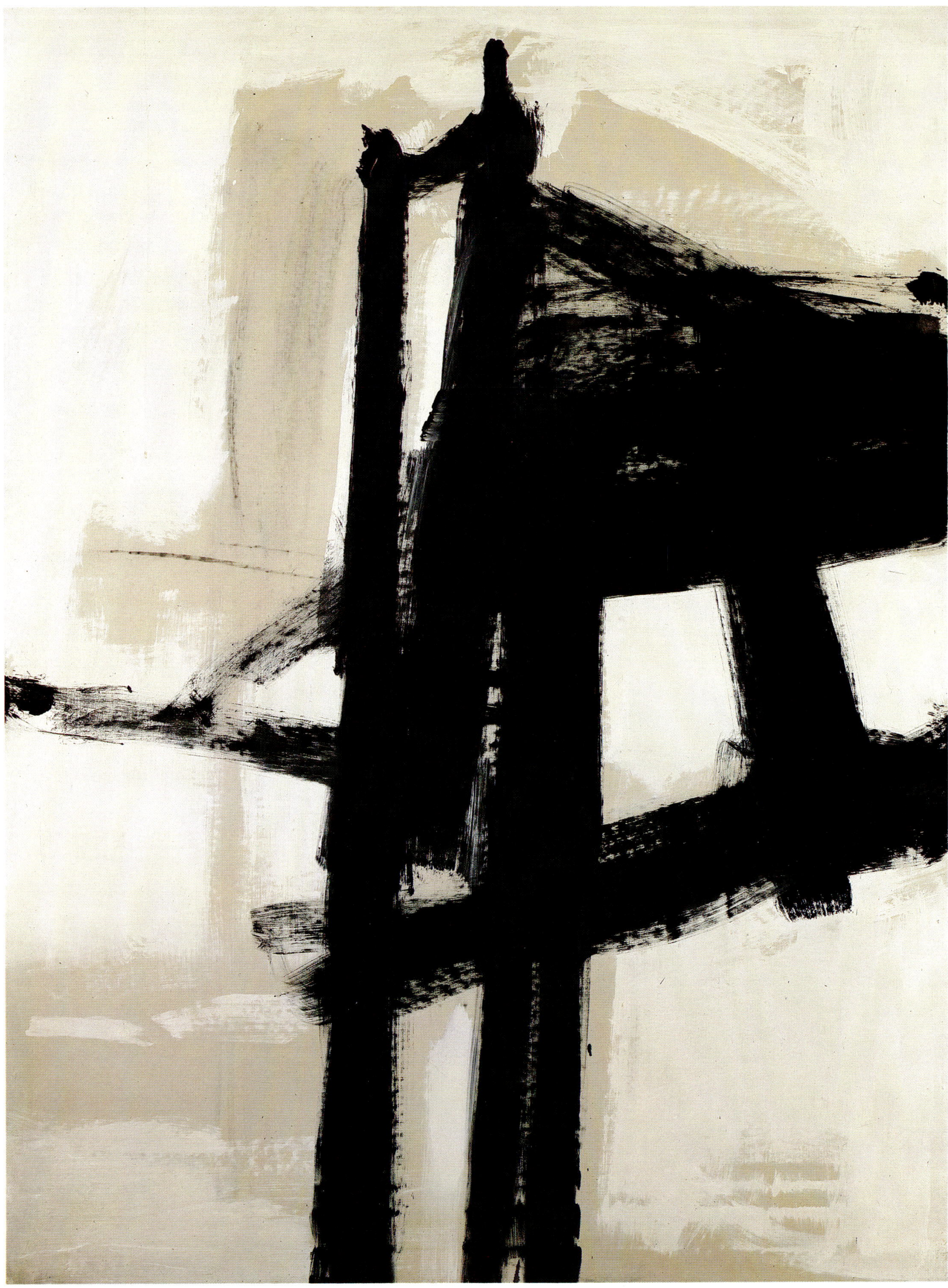

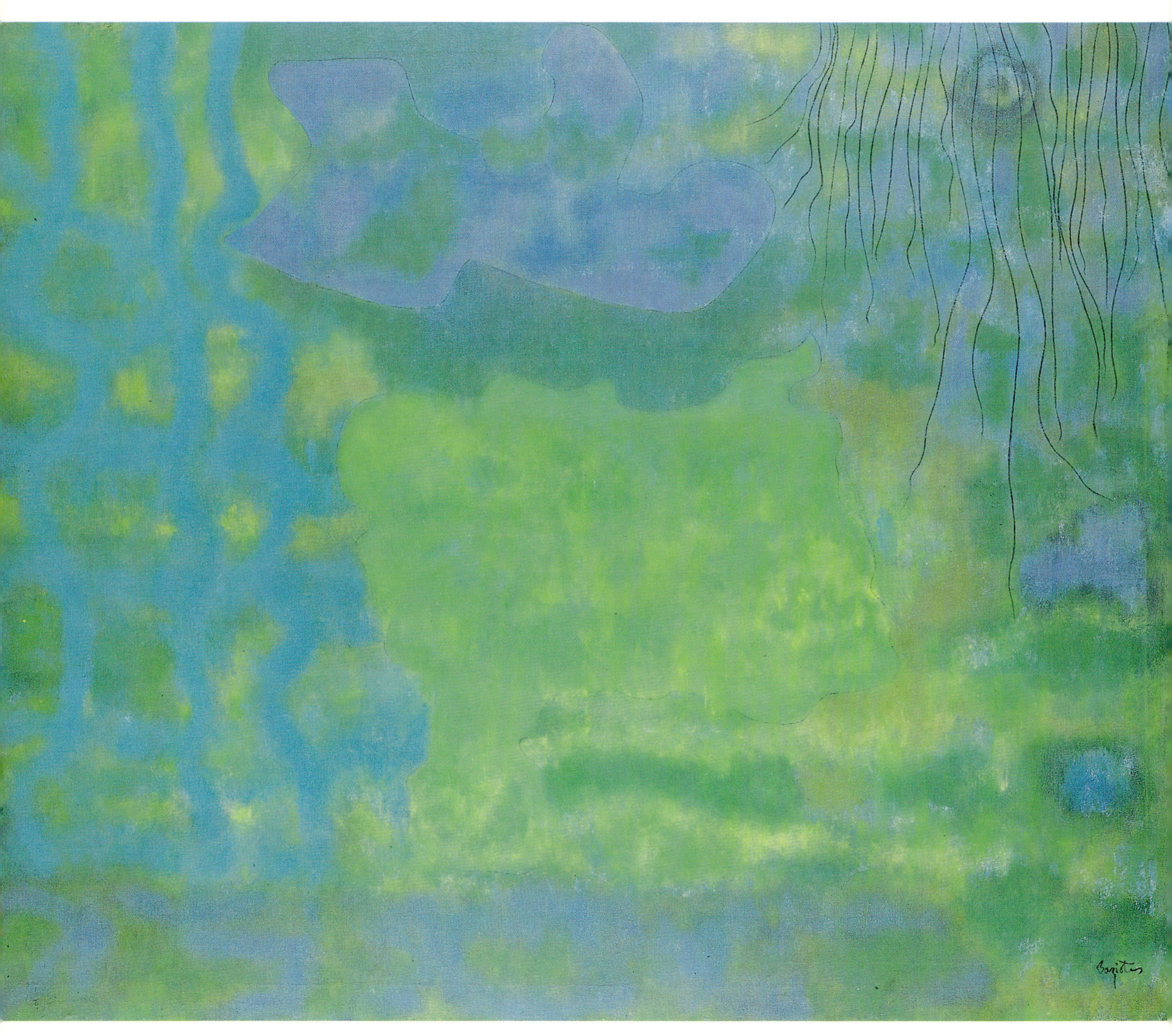

25. William Baziotes
Phantasm, 1951, oil on
canvas.

26. Robert Motherwell
Je T'Aime (I Love You),
1955, oil on canvas.

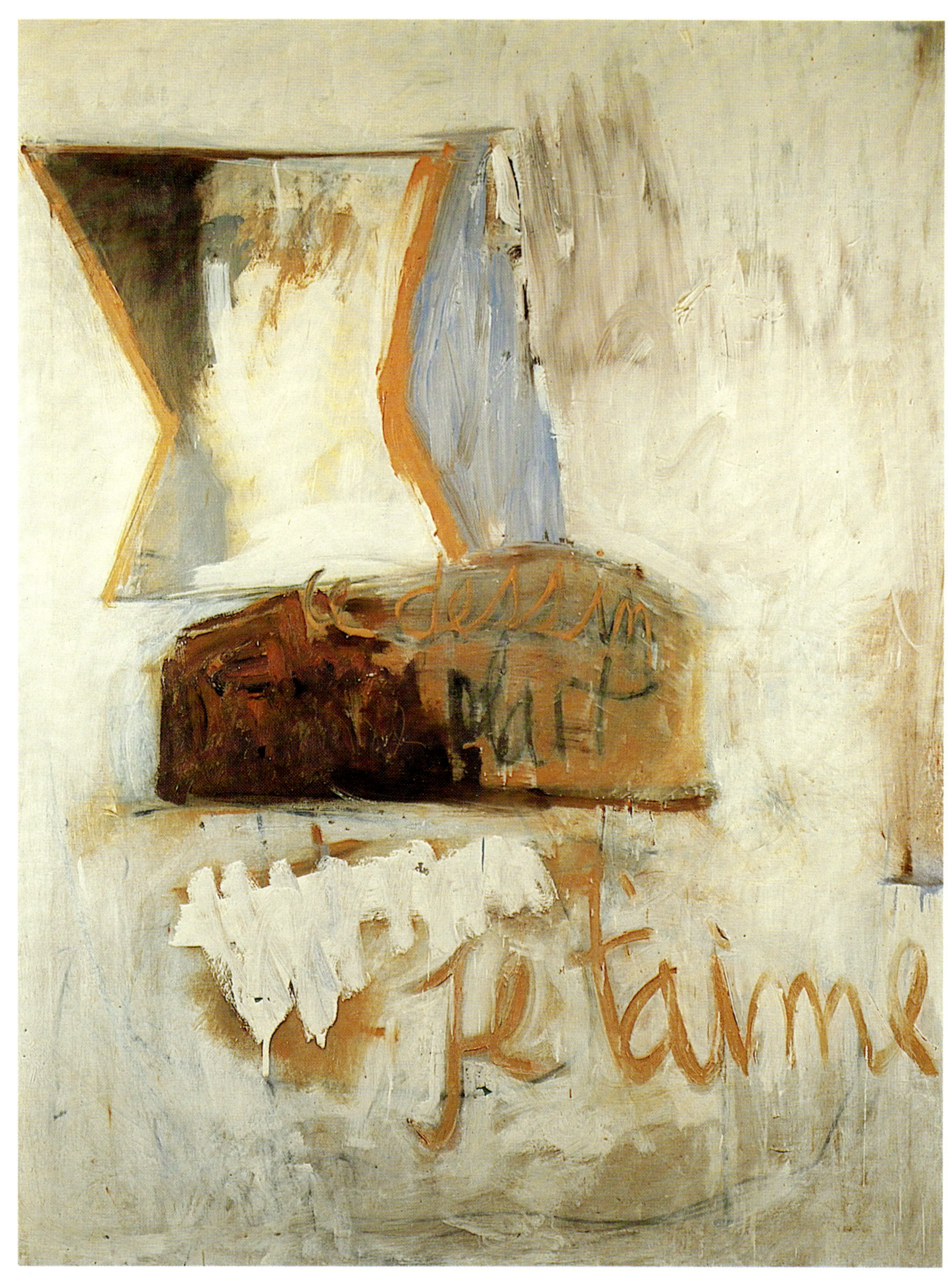

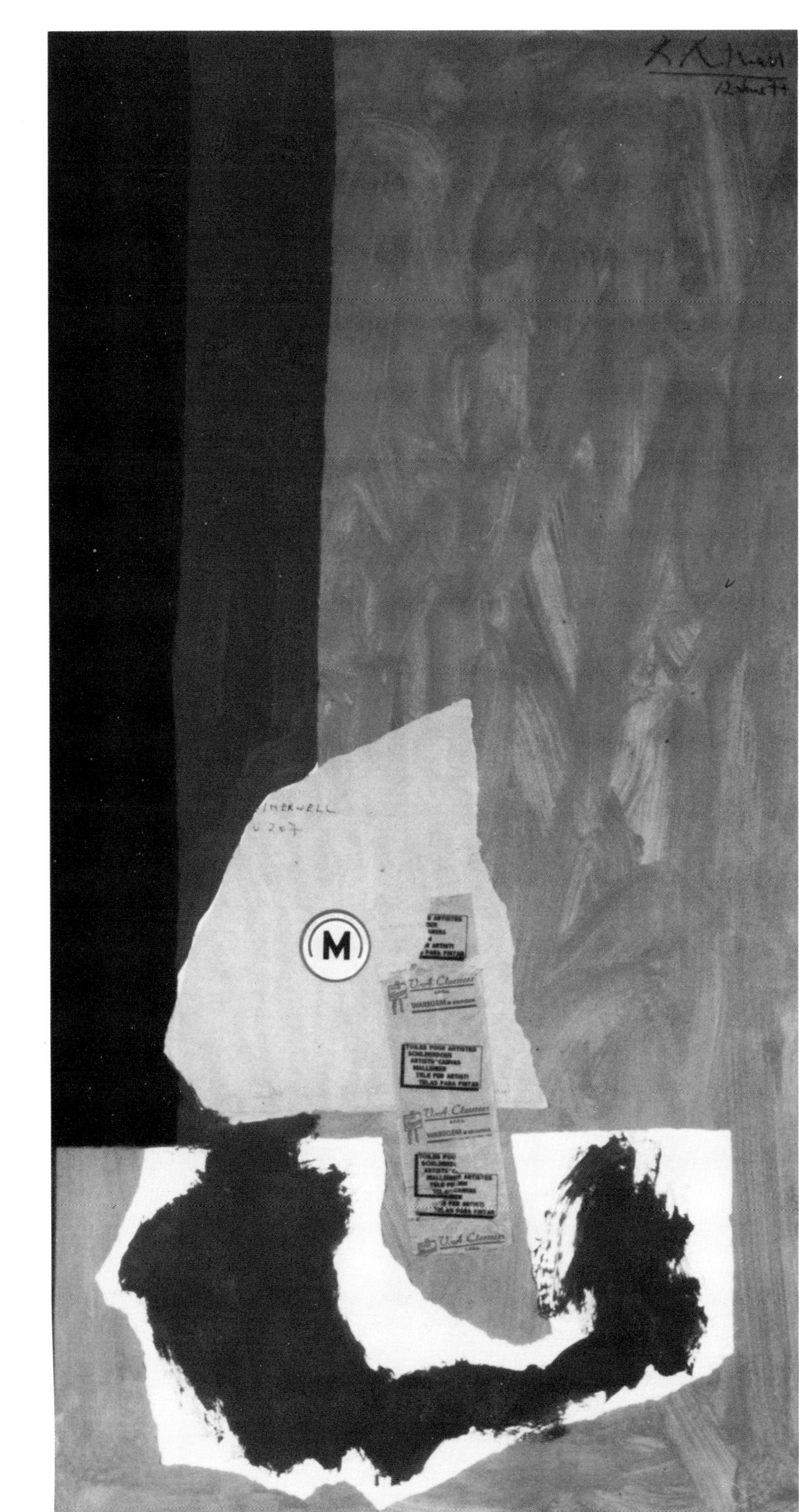

28. Robert Motherwell
Suchard, 1974, collage and
acrylic.

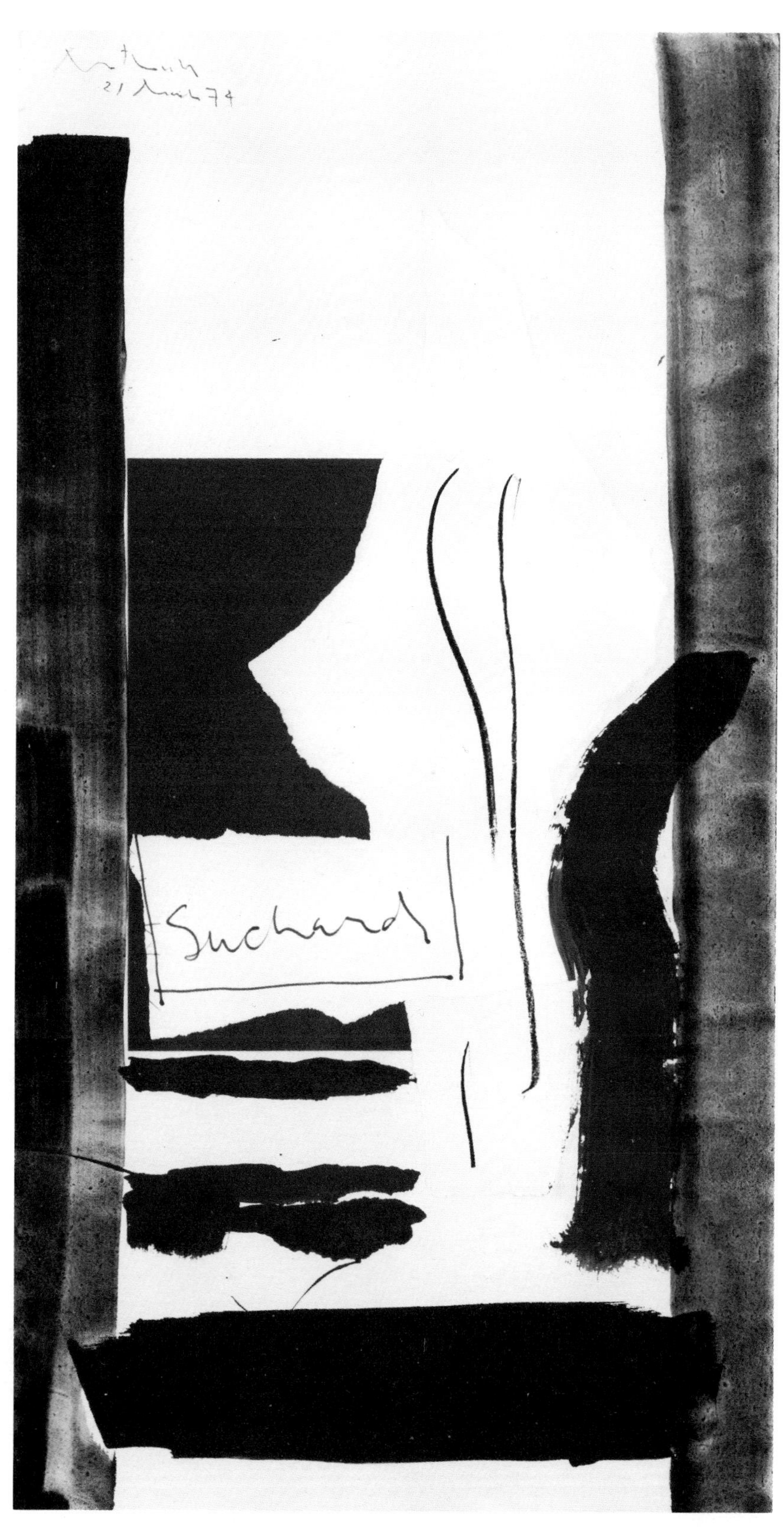

29. Robert Motherwell
XYLOL, 1977, collage on
board.

30. Adolph Gottlieb
Brown Splash, 1970, oil on
canvas.

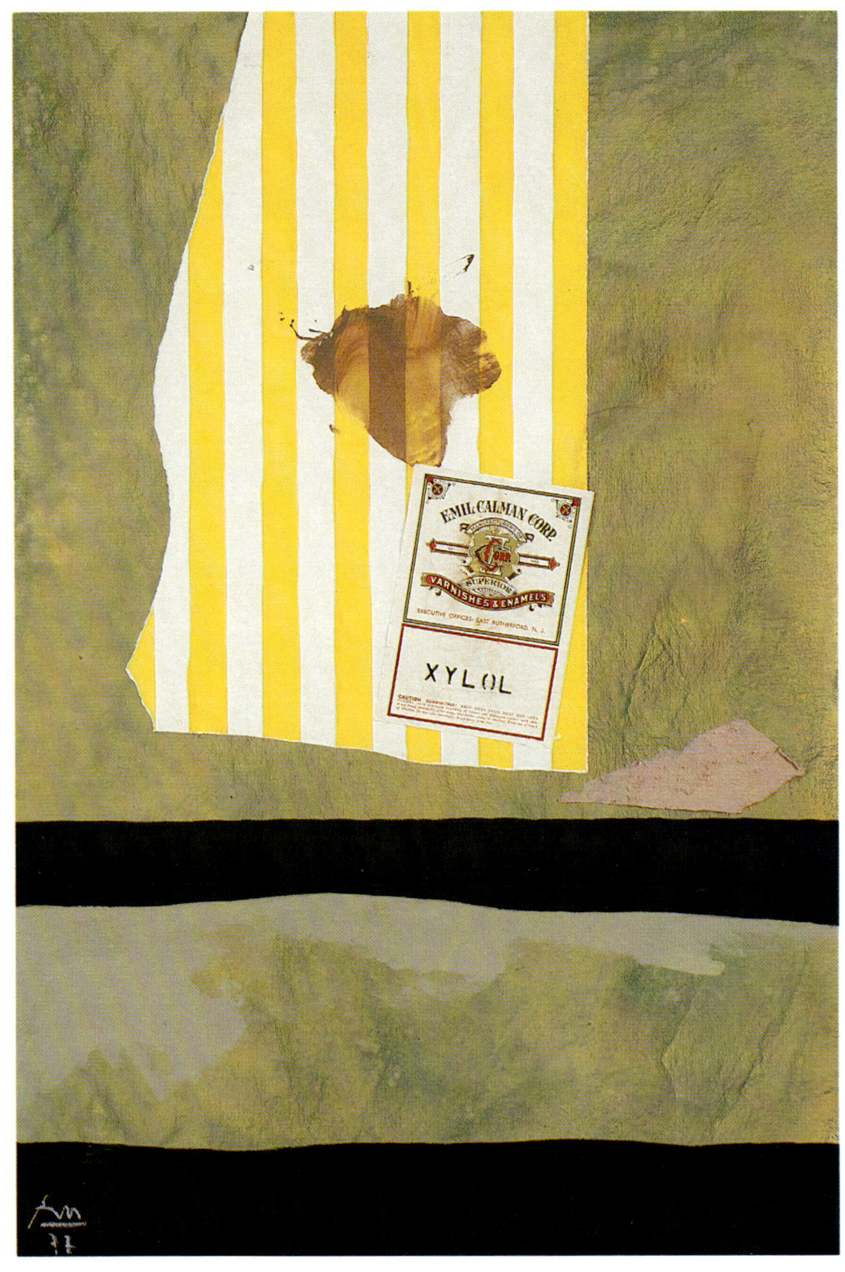

31. David Smith
Volton XXIV, 1963, steel.

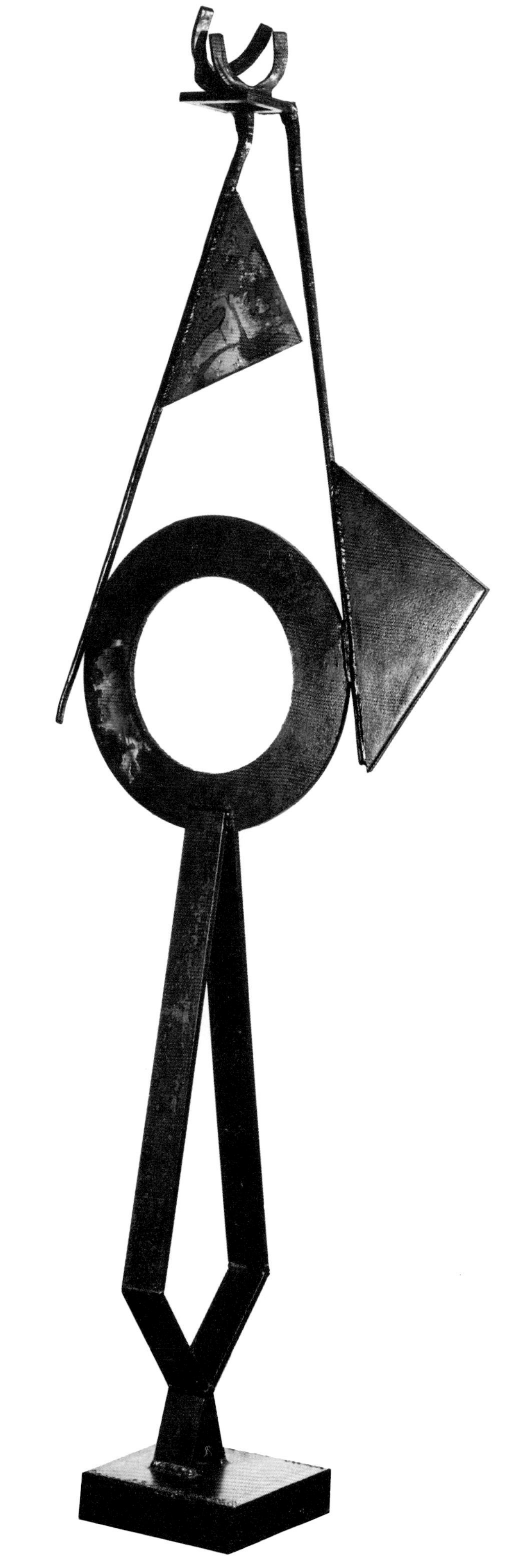

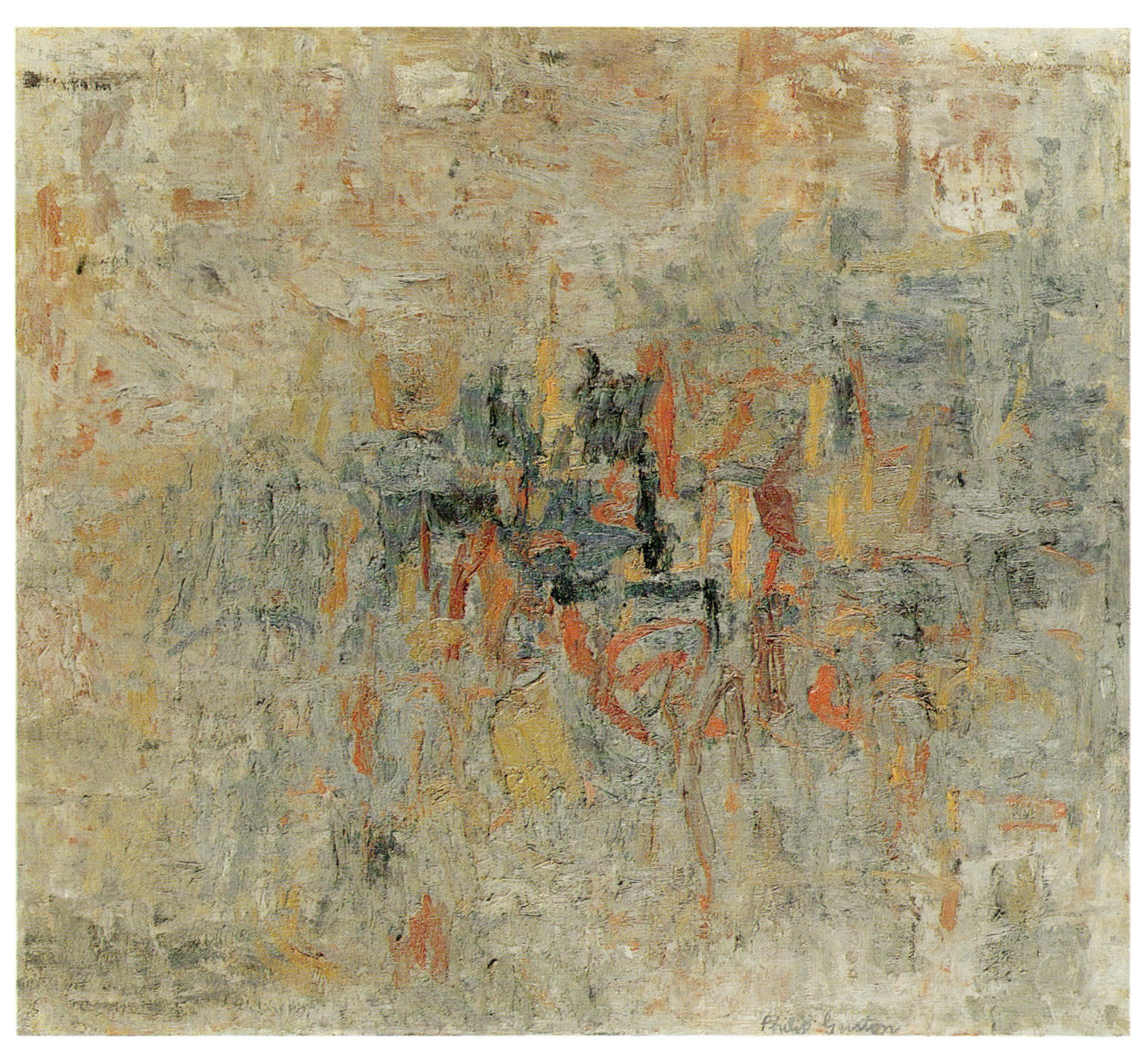

33. Antonio Tapies
No. 10F, 1964, oil and
collage on canvas.

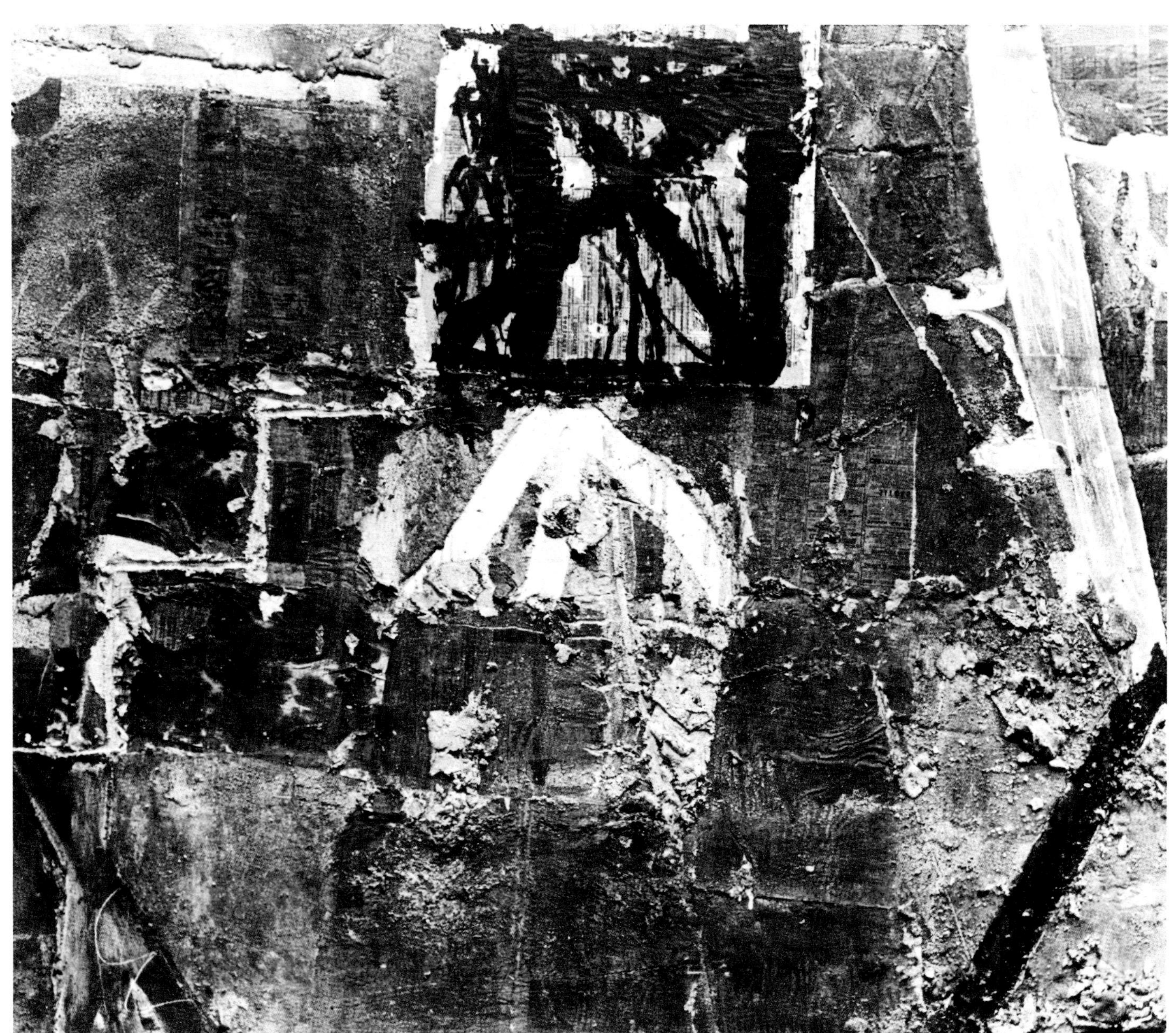

For that power which enables the Artist to conceive his subject with dignity, may be said to belong to general education and is as much the Genius of a Poet, or the professor of any other liberal Art, or even a good critic in any of those arts, as of a Painter.

Sir Joshua Reynolds, *Discourses on Art* (New York: Collier Books, 1966), p. 169.

During the sixties, most of the movements that followed Abstract Expressionism—Color-Field painting, Hard-Edge Abstraction, and Optical Art—abandoned the loaded brush and gestural, autobiographical brushstroke, with their emotional connotations, to concentrate on form and structure. Kenneth Noland, Jules Olitski, Helen Frankenthaler, and the Iranian-born painter Morteza Sazegar belong to the Color-Field movement. Typically, these artists spread or poured thin coats of paint onto unsized canvases so as to stain the fabric and create softly blurred, matte surfaces. The texture of the canvas remains visible, thus obscuring the distinction between figure and ground and emphasizing the surface. Noland's *Warm Reverie* (fig. 34), Olitski's *The Abba's Palace* (fig. 35), Frankenthaler's *Red Support* (fig. 36) and *The Big Dipper* (fig. 37), and Sazegar's *C7-71* (fig. 38) are examples that demonstrate this unity of figure and ground.

Certain painters, including Frank Stella and Agnes Martin, fuse figure and ground, but do so in complex geometrical compositions. The delicate, graphic grids of Martin's mature works, such as *The City* (fig. 40), are wedded to subtly nuanced grounds, thus synthesizing suggestions of stability, tensile strength, and austerity with those of fragility and change. In *Slieve More* (fig. 39), Stella employs a shaped canvas to create a direct, one-to-one correspondence between the image and the physical support of the painting.

Although Louise Nevelson belongs to the same generation as the Abstract Expressionists, her wall sculptures in white, such as *Floating Cloud, Zag II* (fig. 41), seem analogous in mood to Agnes Martin's paintings.

Ellsworth Kelly, Al Held, and Tony King executed hard-edged, intensely colored, geometrical compositions. Held's bold *Untitled No. 1* (fig. 42) is an early, heavily impastoed, painting; *Blue Red* (fig. 43) by Kelly is typical of this artist's deceptively simple compositions that force one's attention to subtle relationships of hue, value, and intensity; while Tony King's *Untitled* (fig. 44) continues, in modified form, the tradition of Op Art.

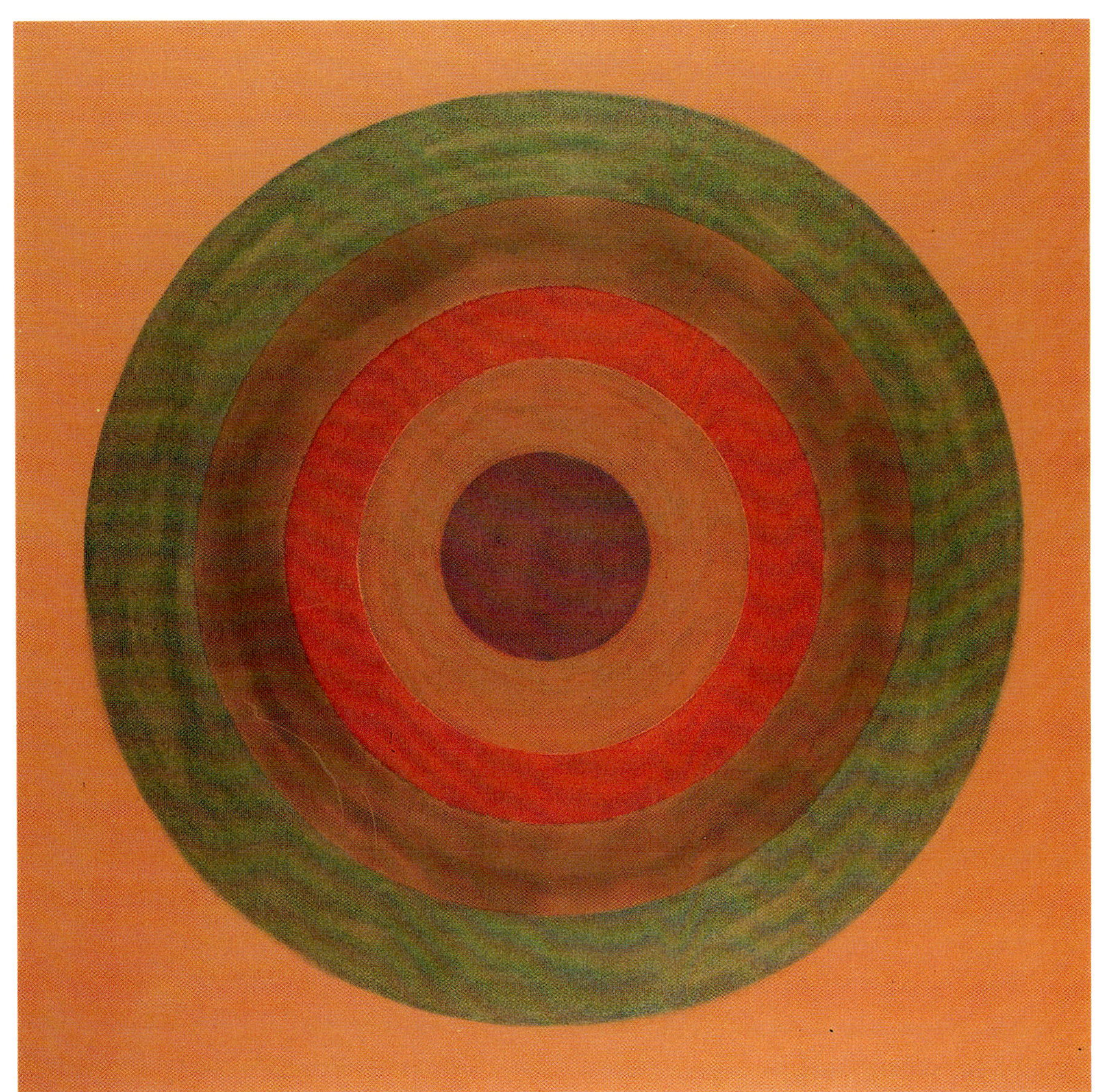

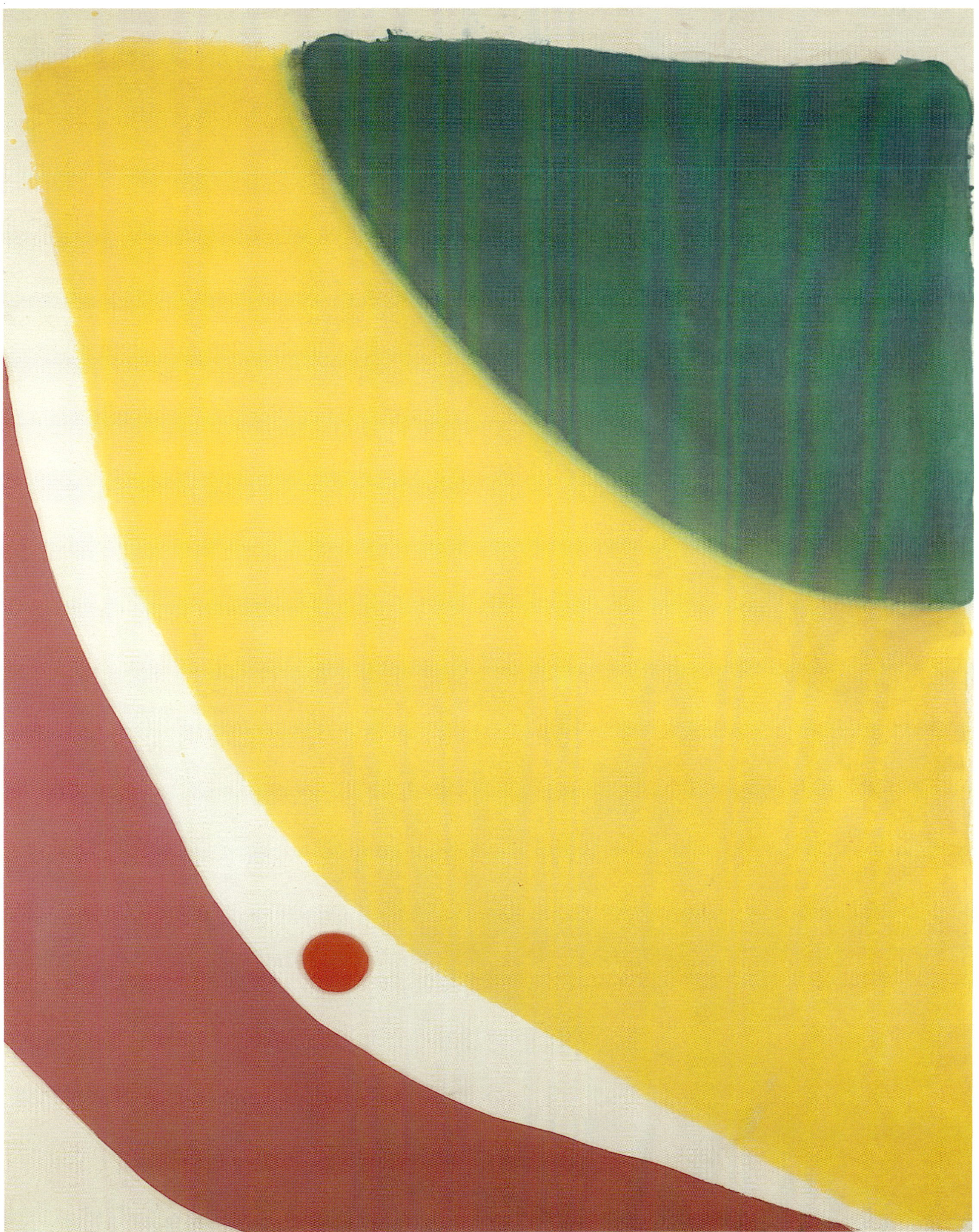

36. Helen Frankenthaler
Red Support, 1964, acrylic
on canvas.

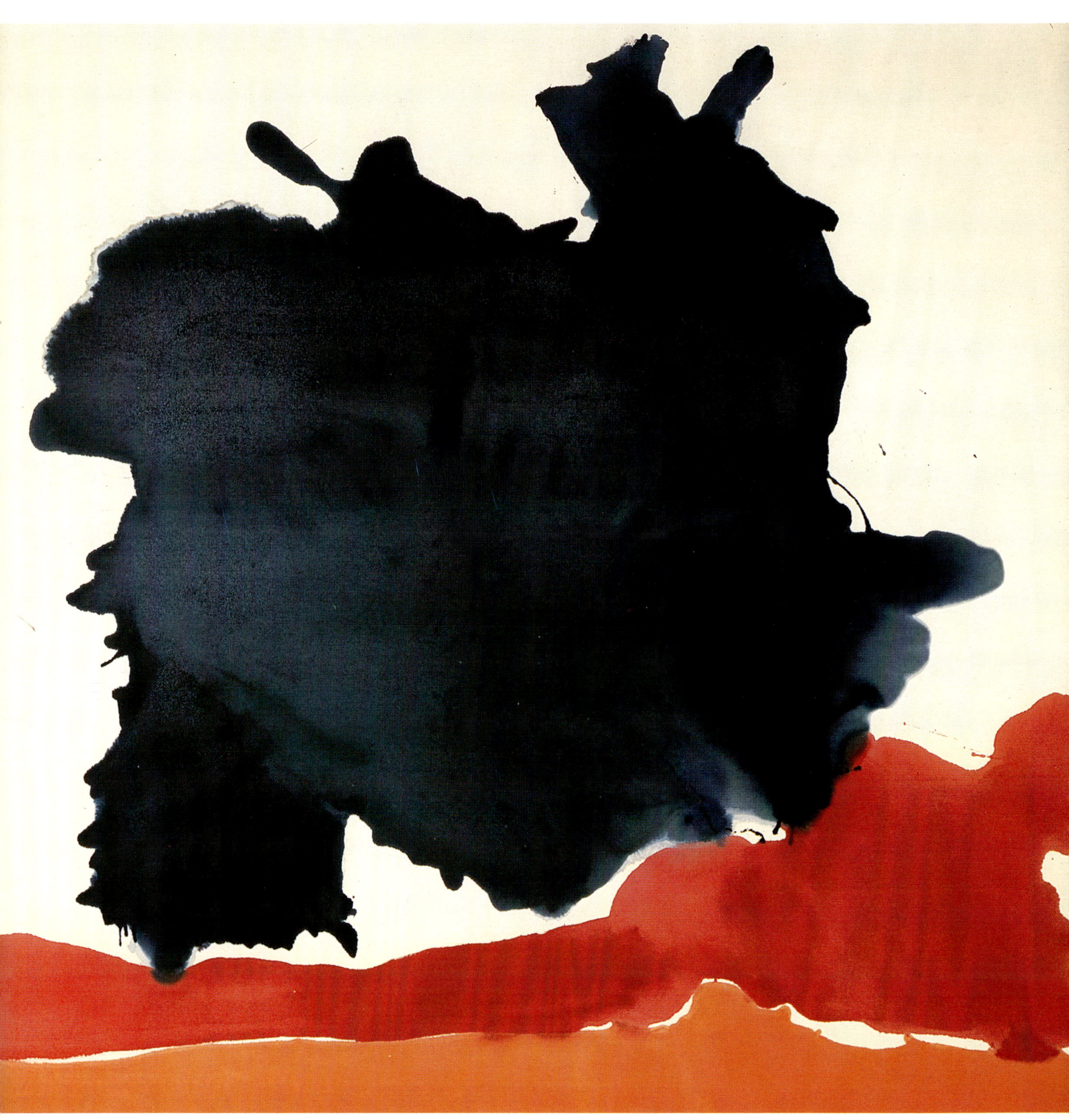

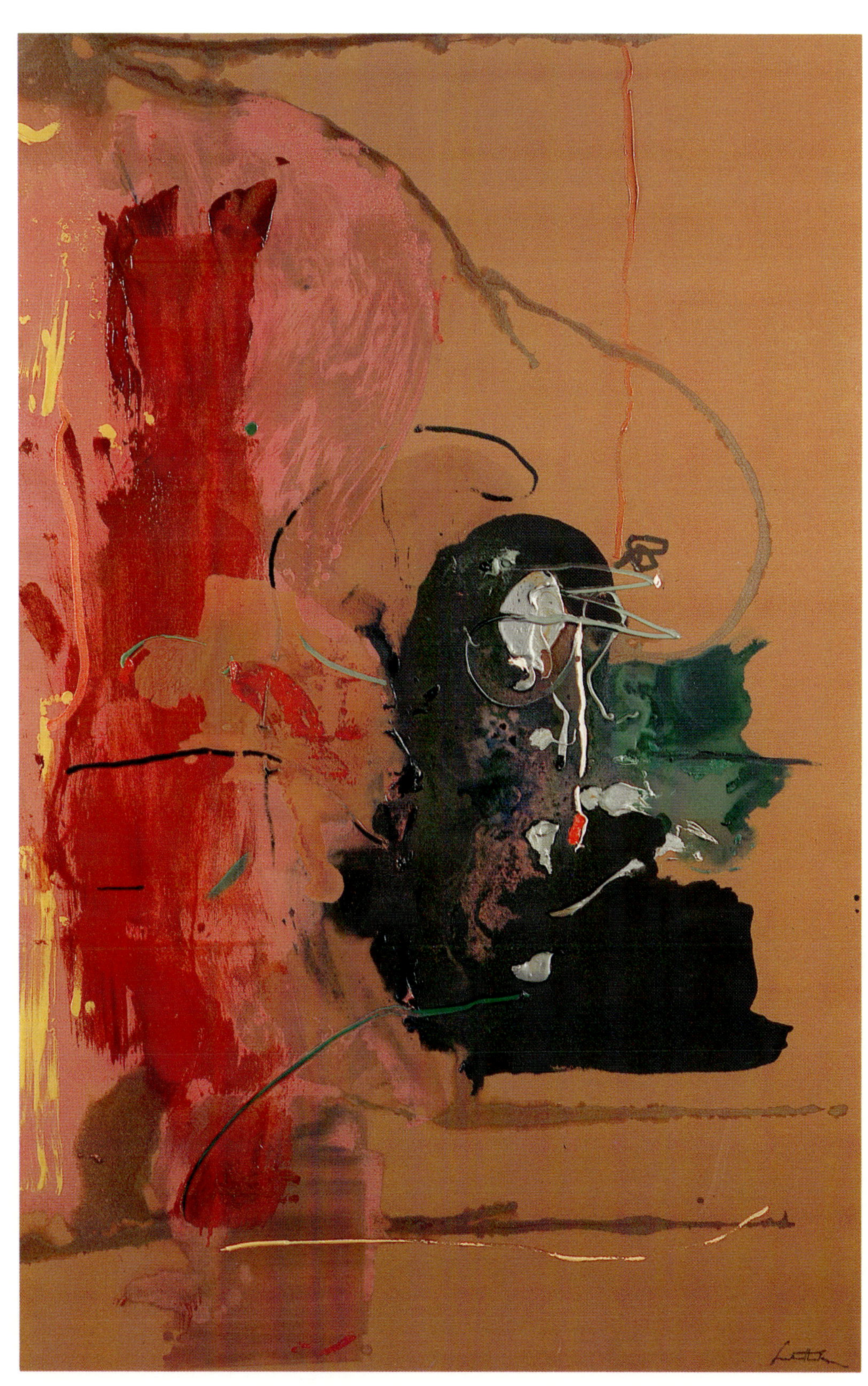

37. Helen Frankenthaler
The Big Dipper, 1985,
acrylic on canvas.

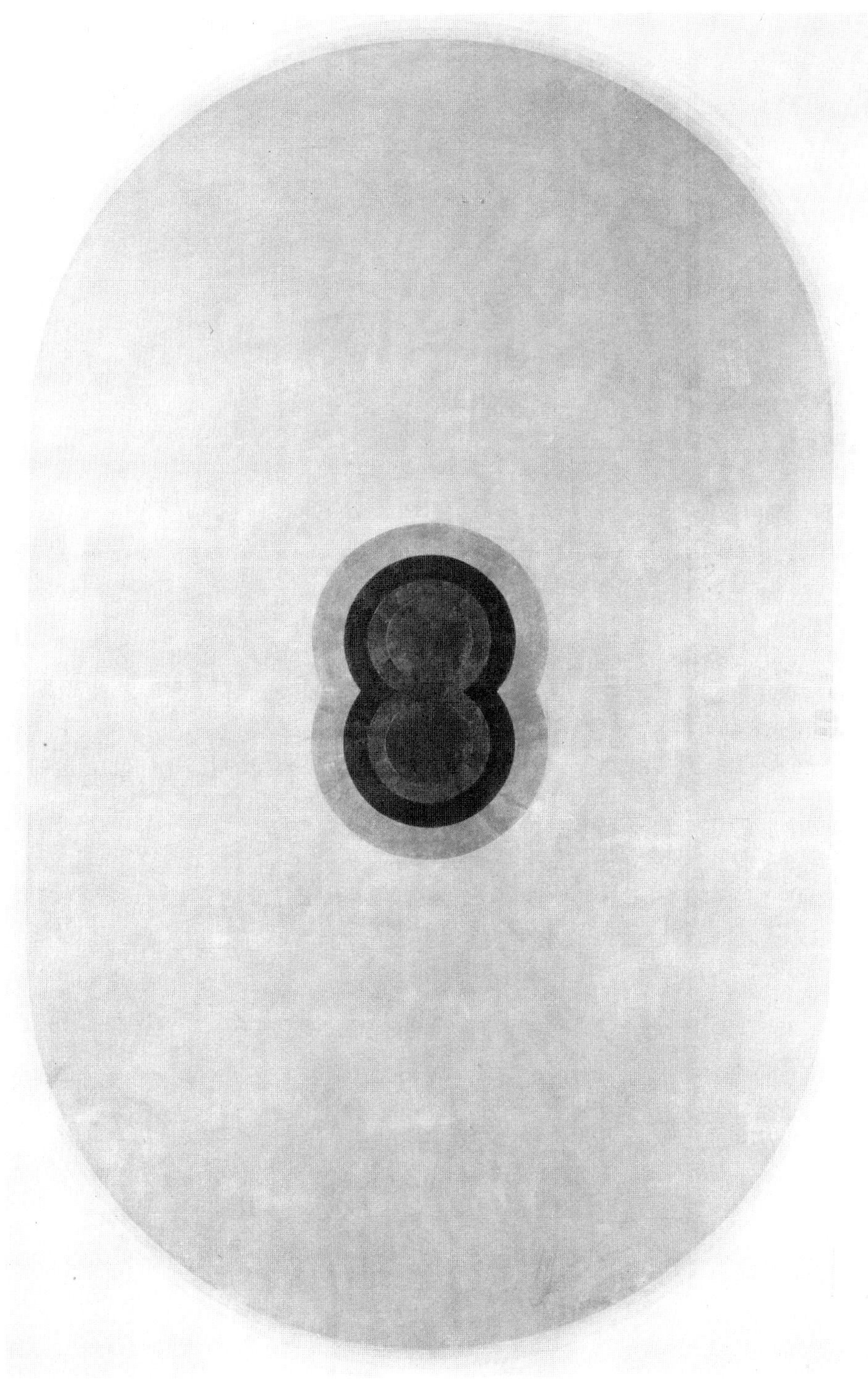

40. Agnes Martin
The City, 1966, acrylic on
canvas.

41. Louise Nevelson
Floating Cloud Zag II, 1977,
painted wood.

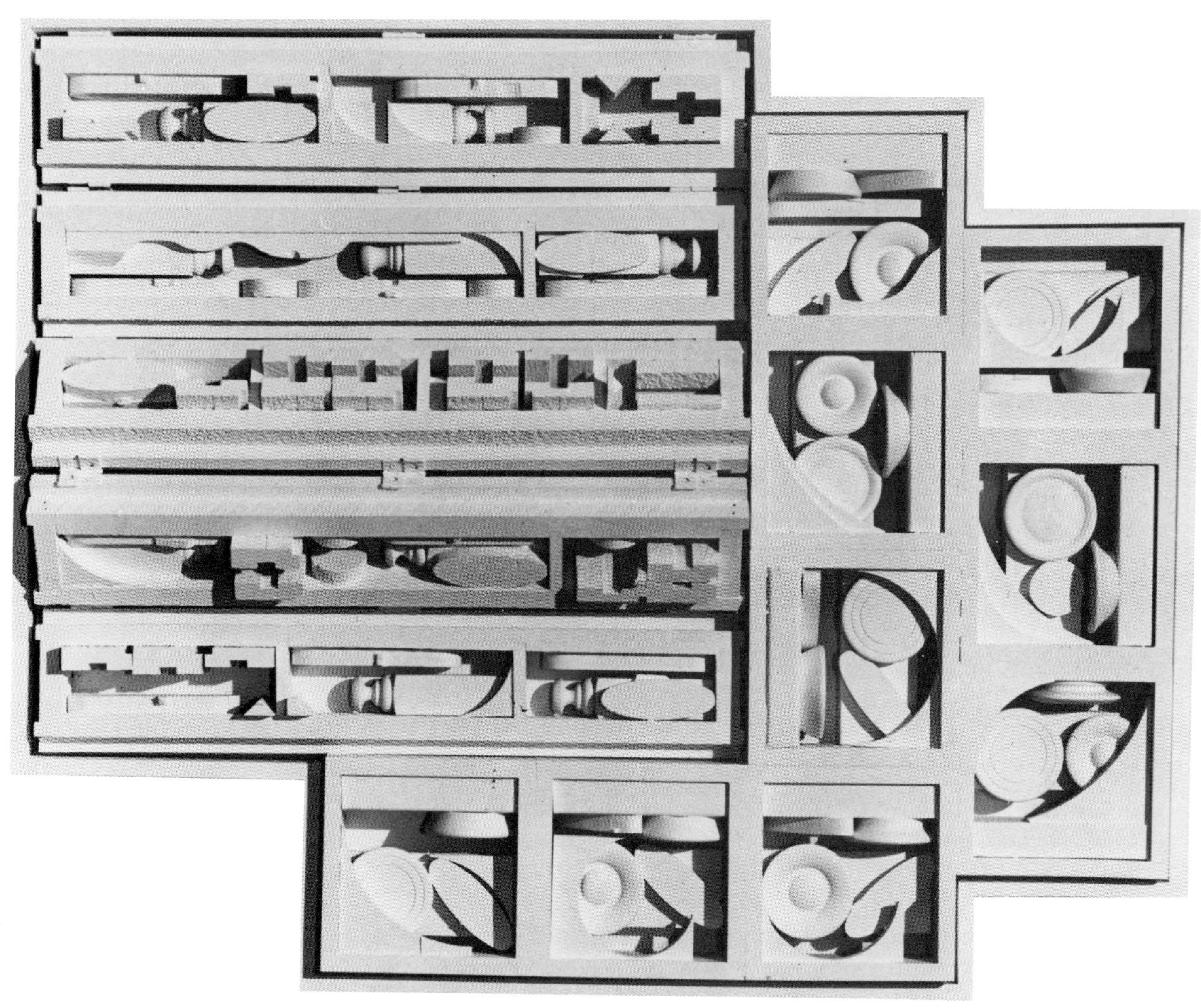

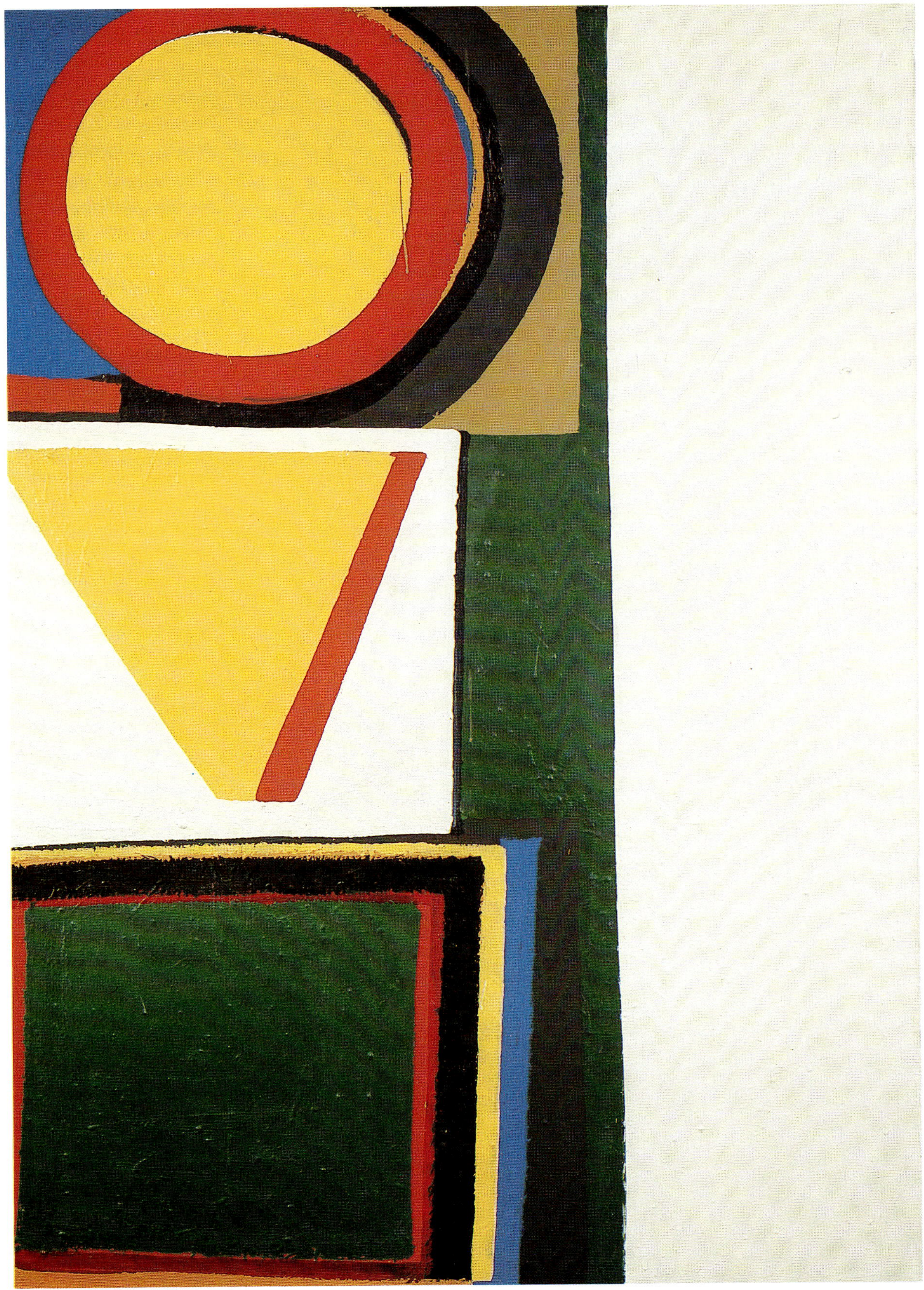

42. Al Held
Untitled No. 1, 1961, acrylic
on canvas.

43. Ellsworth Kelly
Blue Red, 1965, oil on
canvas.

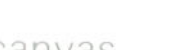

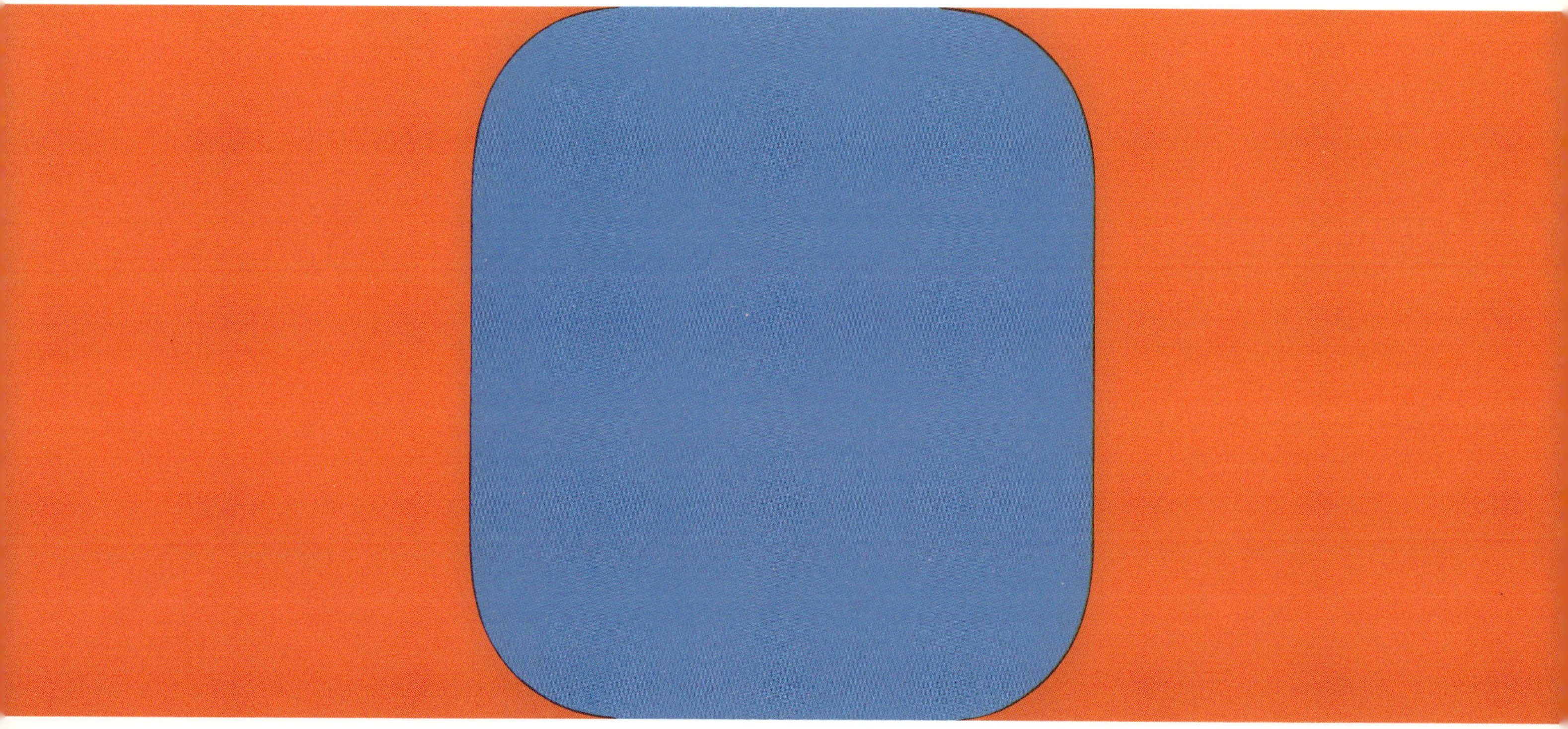

44. Tony King
Untitled, 1979, acrylic on
canvas.

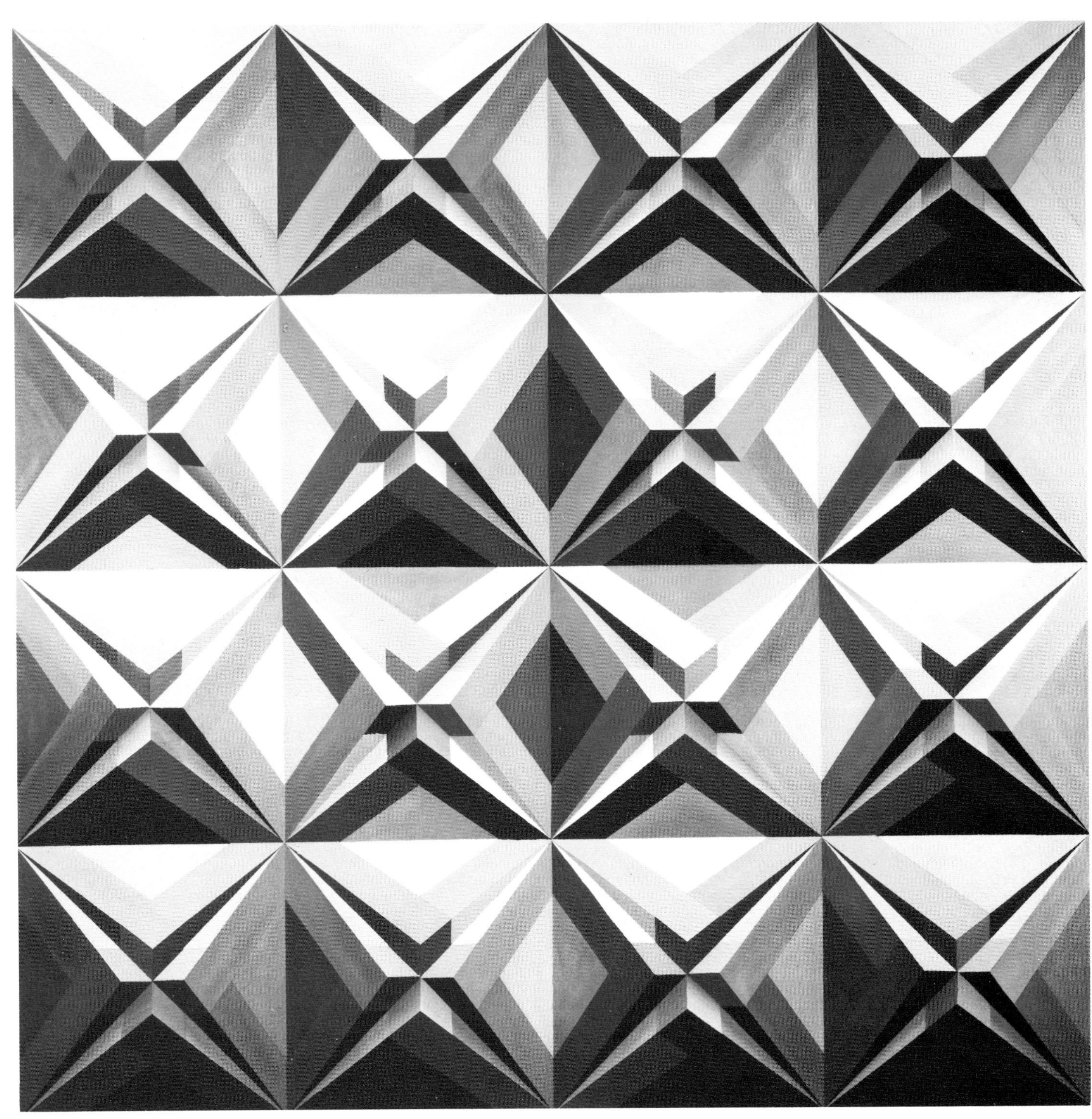

In the seventies, various representational modes reasserted themselves. Philip Guston's last, ''brutal'' style appears to have influenced many younger artists; after the fifties Guston's art had evolved toward a more somber, anxious mood, and by the late sixties he had returned to figurative imagery—as in *Entrance* (fig. 45)—depicting shoes, clocks, hooded figures, and eyes in a grotesque style remotely related to certain old comic strips. Far from being humorous, however, these paintings convey bleak despair.

Georg Baselitz continues the German Expressionist tradition with direct application of thick pigment and raw, dark colors, as in *Stilleben* (fig. 46). His upside-down images startle the viewer into a heightened state of awareness and emphasize form over subject.

Frank Auerbach renders his figures and landscapes—*Primrose Hill* (fig. 47), for example—with a vigorous and heavily loaded brush. The expressive character of his work derives from its spontaneous informality and the way in which pigment is manipulated as if it were a plastic material.

R. B. Kitaj is an incisive draftsman who uses broad areas of thin, clear hues to carefully develop his compositions, as in *Starting a War* (fig. 48). He takes his subjects from literature, history, and philosophy to make contemporary social comments. His friend David Hockney is also a strong draftsman and designer; his portrait drawings, however—such as *Ann Reading* (fig. 49)—skillfully capture the character of his sitters.

Alfred Leslie presents another aspect of the new, representational painting. Looking to such old masters as Caravaggio, Georges de La Tour, and Gerrit van Honthorst, he developed dramatically composed and lighted compositions, like *Instant Pictures* (fig. 50), which use these elements as well as narrative content to explore the moral problems of contemporary society.

45. Philip Guston
Entrance, 1979, oil on
canvas.

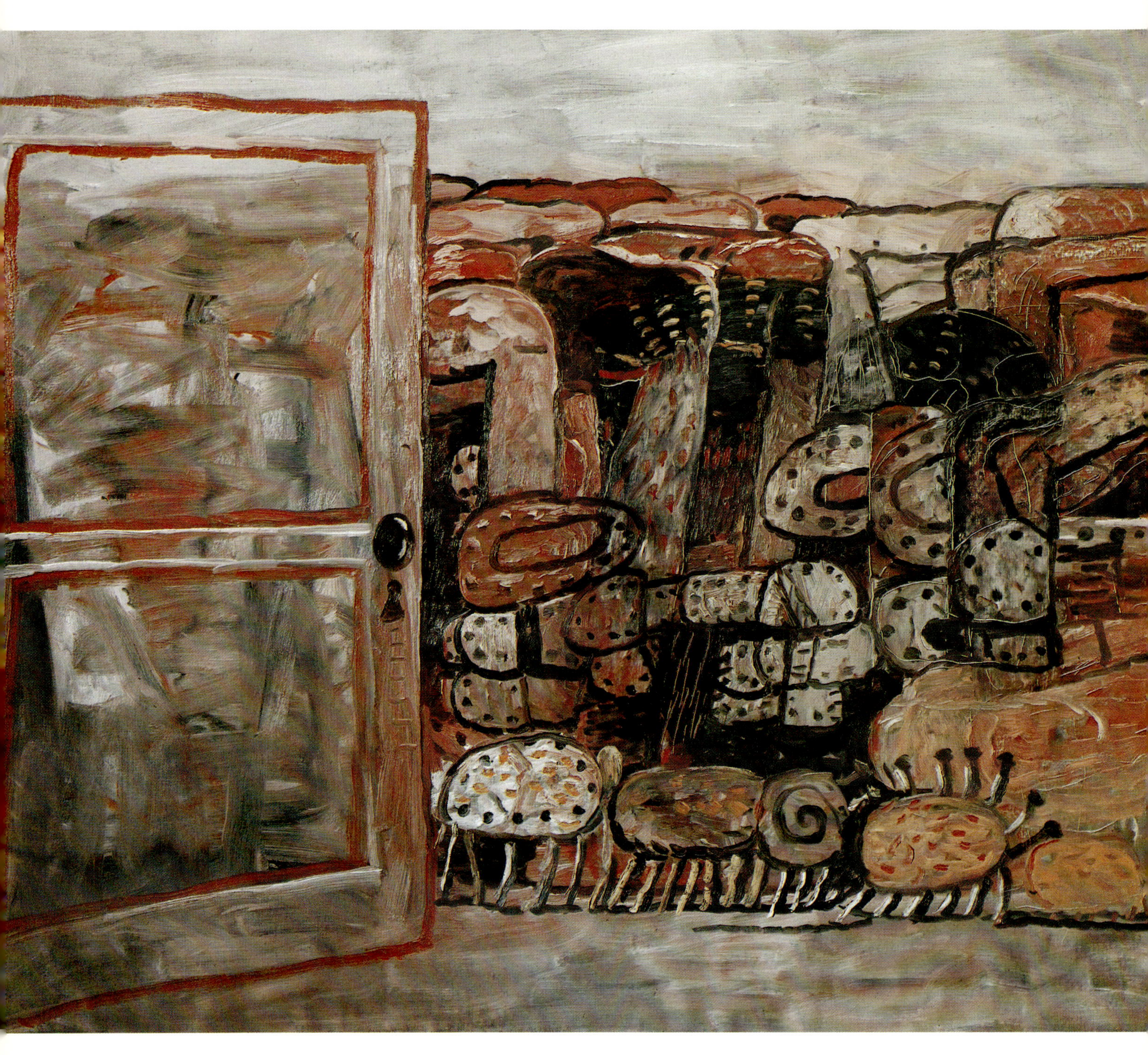

46. Georg Baselitz
Stilleben (*Still Life*),
1976-77, acrylic on canvas.

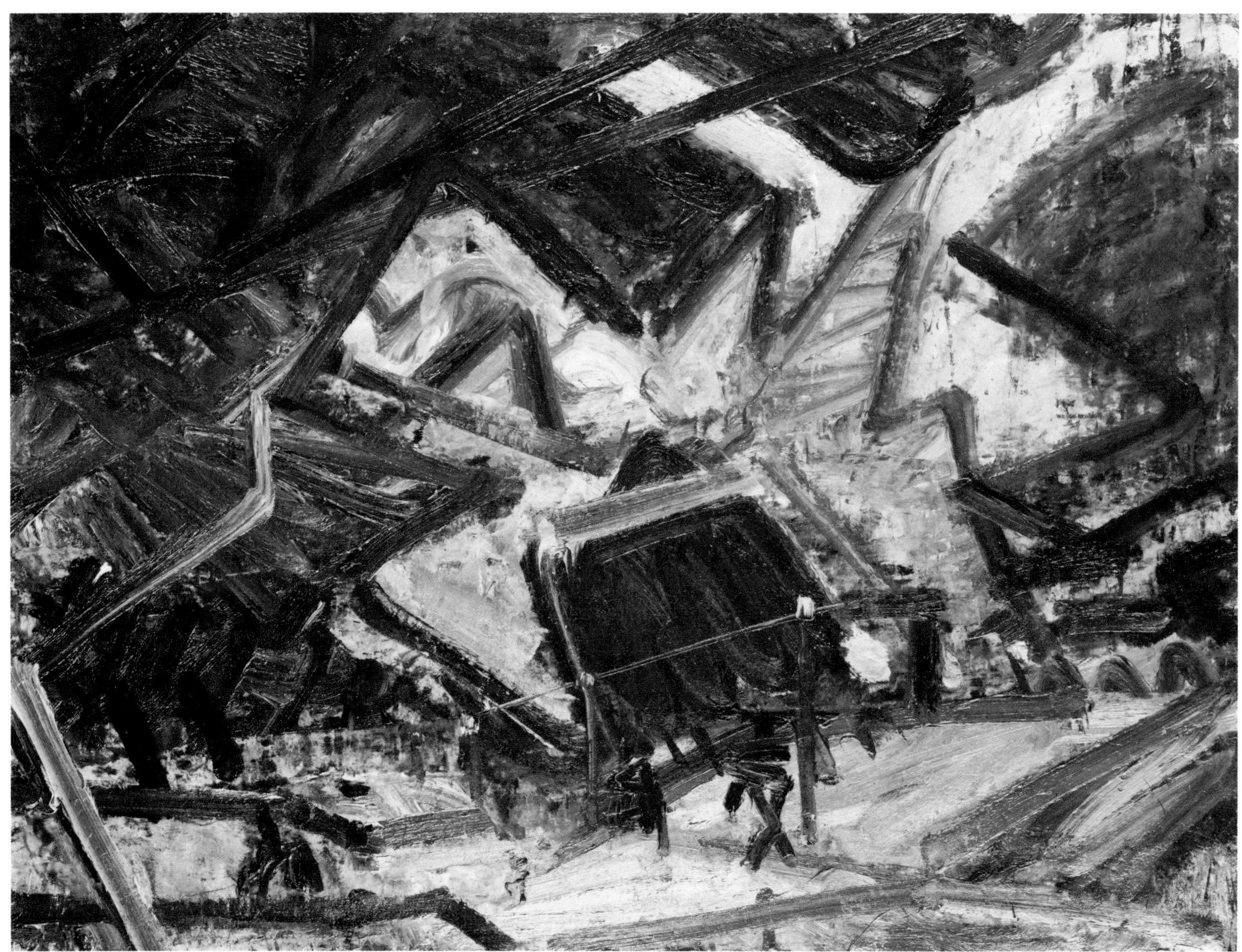

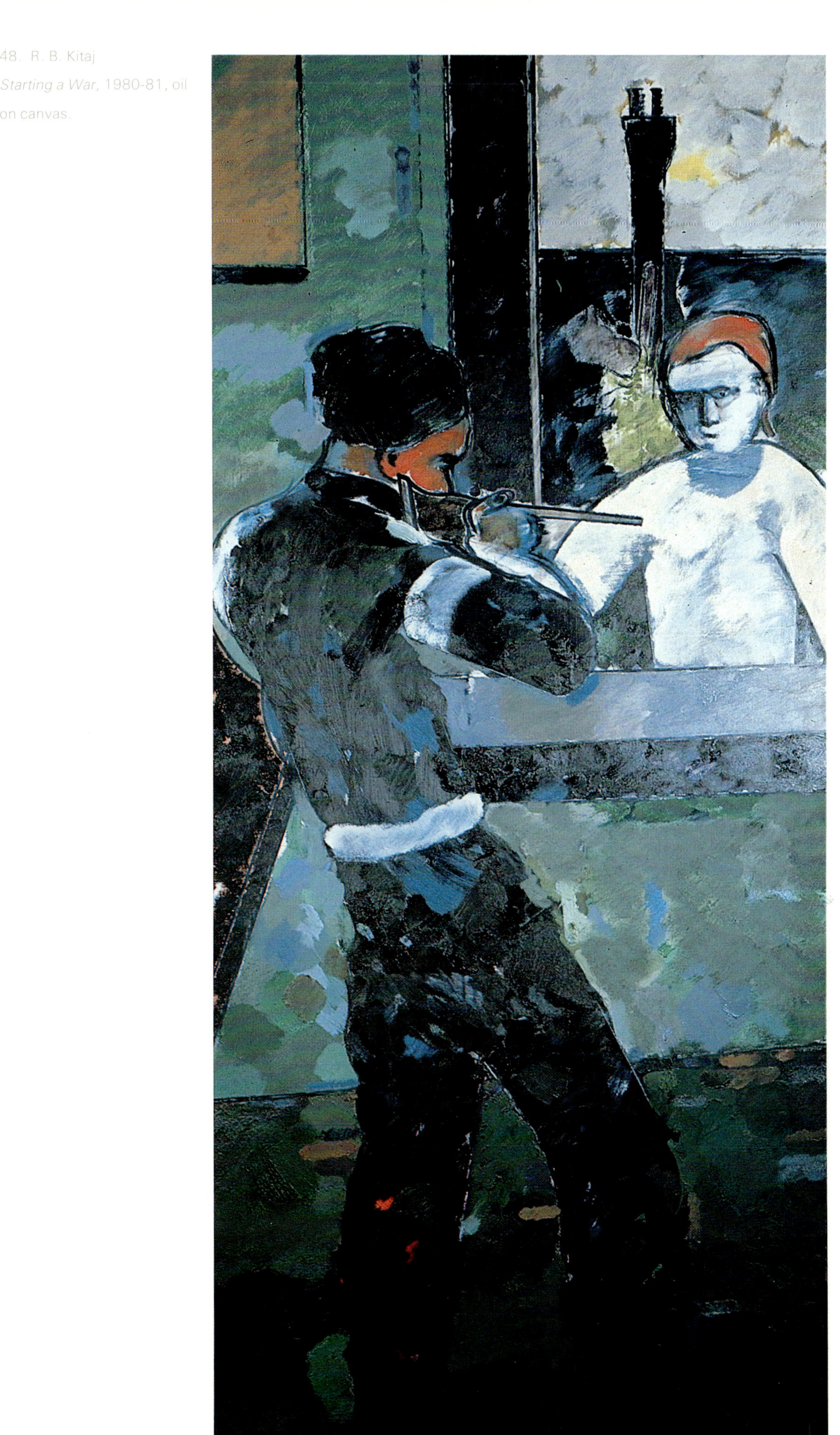

48. R. B. Kitaj
Starting a War, 1980-81, oil
on canvas.

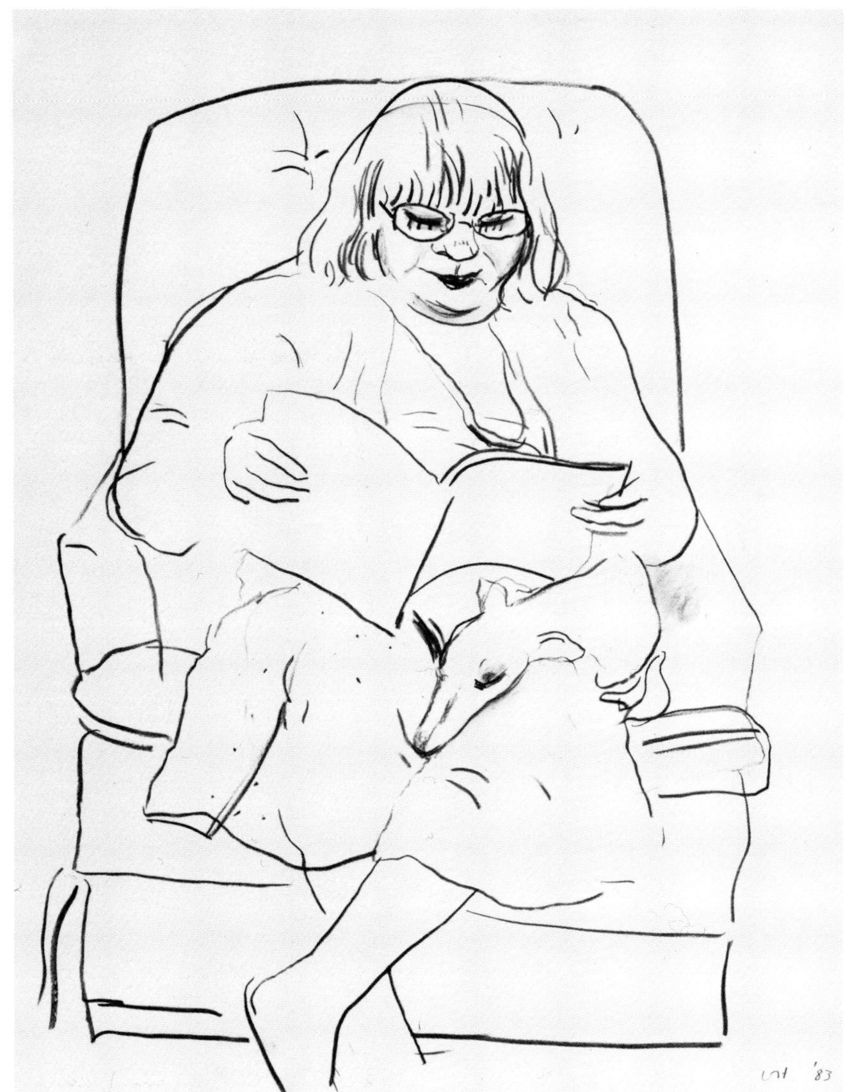

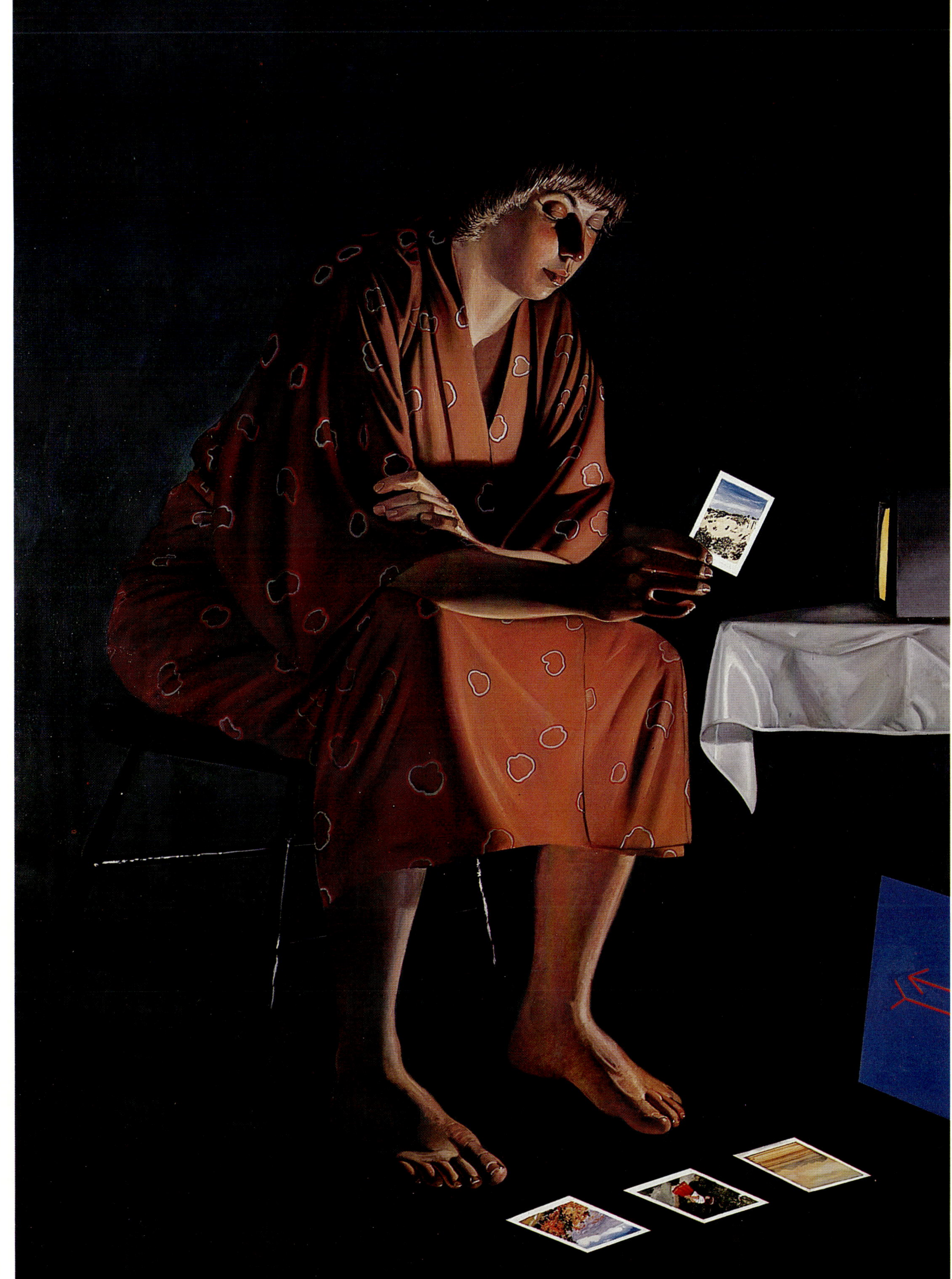